Ron –
Best wishes from
george,

# Golden Years My Ass

# Golden Years My Ass
## Adventures in Geriatric Indignity

By Roger Welsch

ISBN: 978-0-557-63801-7

Disclaimer: Any resemblance of events and persons in this book to actual persons living or dead is completely coincidental. Really. Take my word of it. I mean, look at this stuff: would any actual person 1) survive all of this woe, 2) make this many dumb mistakes, or 3) then tell the world about it? Would you believe me if I told you I had sex with Venus and Serena Williams? Both? At the same time? And lived?! Get serious! All of the stories here are true, mostly, but we have a rule in the little town where I live that we can improve on a fish story 10% with each telling, and believe me, I've told most of these stories a lot of times. So figure it out. The geographic locations mentioned here have been changed and mixed up, the hospitals and clinics gossiped about are cleverly and completely disguised, the doctors are no one you know, and believe me, the sexy, trash-talking nurses and hot techies are not your wife. I'm not even sure I am real, now that I think about it. So relax and stop trying to figure out who everyone in this book is. You're wrong. That's not the person you know. It's someone else. It's definitely not you!

*For Mom, who has made my senior years miserable by being stronger, sprier, and cheerier at 96 than I am at 73. She left us just five days ago as I write these words. My father died a death in keeping with his spirit…in his last cogent moments he told Mom he loved her, he made us laugh, and he flirted with a nurse. Mom did the same: her last words were, "Linda, go home" because she didn't want to disrupt our schedule or inconvenience anyone with her dying. That was my mother.*

*"I can't imagine why my body is letting me down now after I have devoted my entire life to keeping it happy."*

*Roger Welsch, Golden Ager*

# TABLE OF CONTENTS:

A FOREWORD:                                          ix

A BRIEF SUMMARY OF MY HEALTH CHART:                  1

GOLDEN YEARS MY ASS...                               7

MAINTENANCE AND REPAIRS...                           27

THE HEART OF THE MATTER:                             43

THE BIG C:                                           73

LIFESTYLES OR MAYBE NOT:                             105

CUTTING THE LIFELINE:                                109

ACCIDENT PRONE, PRONE ACCIDENTS, ETC.                121

COMMON AND OTHER SENSES:                             135

MISC HEALTH:                                         147

SOLUTIONS:                                           161

An afternote—                                        189

# A FOREWORD:

Forty years ago I was strolling the back streets of Bad Kreutznach, a beautiful, small town on the Rhine River, when an ancient, leaning, crumpled, bent, sagging, old, half-timber house caught my eye. Its antiquity was obvious. It had obviously been lovingly restored but still showed every curve, bend, sag, crack, and flaw of its centuries-old front wall. Iron supports and steel ties extended from some of the timbers, clearly intended to keep the building from simply falling into the street. Concrete buttresses and iron beams offered support around its exterior…God only knows what devices had been installed in the building's interior to keep it standing. I took some photos, however, because it really was a remarkable old building.

Through the telephoto lens of my camera I spotted a small porcelain plate attached to a beam maybe twelve or fifteen feet off the sidewalk. The writing on it was so small, I had to get as close as I could to the bulging wall and then strain to read it. It took me a while but eventually I figured out the inscription: "Auch ich war einmal jung und schoen…" "I too was once young and handsome…" I laughed, and got a shot of the amusing little sign to add to my tourist album. Pretty funny... "I too was once young and handsome..."

Over the years I've thought about that building and its quiet, gentle declaration to passersby...more often now, it seems, than I did before. The words are not so much an apology as a caution. Yes, I too was once and beautiful but...eventually you too will be ancient and bent like me. I never forgot that sign or the building it was affixed to. And now the time has come when I can honestly and even triumphantly say the same thing. What I thought was funny in my youth has become poignant now, and yet all the more true. I wish I had a T-shirt or jacket with that little sign embossed subtly somewhere on one of the shoulders. I imagine my increasing interest in what the ancient building told me comes partially from my growing knowledge of how that building intended to end its sentence: "Once I too was young and handsome...[but now I am old and interesting]."

No, I am no longer young and beautiful, but I can't say with any honesty that I am any less enthusiastic or appreciative about life, or feel much loss in my pleasure that like that old building I am still standing... battered, bombed, strafed, scarred, worn, abused, propped up, bolstered, propped, re-enforced, bolted, strapped, restored, braced, refurbished...but still standing, no longer young and handsome, but, by God, old and hopefully still interesting.

Those of you who are old like me and read what I have written here will nod and laugh because you know exactly what I am saying. You are here too. Nothing I am saying is new to you but what I have written is something of an affirmation for you; for those of you who have the Golden Years ahead of you, well, let this be not a warning but a note of gentle caution. There's no avoiding it. You are going to get old too. And you can accept that and laugh along with me, or you can futilely resist and fight the inevitable. You can sag and bend and lean and become interesting like that ancient structure I saw in Bad Kreuznach, or you can patch and paint, redecorate, and modernize your surface and be laughed at like all those pathetic Hollywood stars who fight the years and wind up looking like they accidentally stumbled into a hive of angry bees and have swoll up like an inflatable parade balloon.

That's not for me. This is me. Every crag, scar, dent and divot is original and real. The closest I have come to cosmetic surgery is when Lovely Linda has had enough and attacks my ear hair with a weed whacker. And what you read here is true too. I'm not bragging. My medical trials are not heroic or the least bit unusual. Every time I undergo a new "procedure," I find that most of my contemporaries (a nice word for "cronies") have had the same issues, or something even better. ("You have a PaceMaker? Big deal! I have two bypasses, four stents, an ablation, and three catheterizations! And talk about kidney stones?! They are the <u>worst!</u>")

So don't expect to learn much in these pages. Don't expect any spiritual guidance or goofy feel-fuzzy commiseration. There's not going to be a lot of comfort here, at least no phony crap suggesting that all you have to do is cheer up and everything will be fine. It won't. I won't lie to you: you're going to get sick, hurt, and humiliated. That's the nature of getting old. You'll get damn tired of it, and chances are a lot of people will get damn tired of you getting tired of it. And then you'll die. We all do. As I like to say, "You live and you learn. Then you die and forget it all."

# A BRIEF SUMMARY OF MY HEALTH CHART:

I haven't always been a stove-up old geezer, you know. I am not puny by inclination, disposition, or genetics. A few weeks ago some misguided soul invited me to speak at a local health fair on the topic of "holistic health." "Easy enough," I said. "Suck it up and move along. There you are…my approach to holistic health." In my long life I have only rarely been badly sick or severely injured. I had the usual set of childhood problems…chicken pox, mumps, ear problems, colds…and in my adolescence I came down with the health problems that characterize that stage of life: surliness, obsessions with various parts of girls (especially a couple of girls who sat ahead of me in history class and were constantly walking back and forth to the blackboard, thus obliterating any possibility I might otherwise have learned something about history), acne, acute lack of coordination, stuttering in the presence of girls, and the total inability to dance.

I'm German so when I had health issues I usually just swallowed hard, toughed it out, and marched straight ahead into the bayonets of the enemy. For fifty years I could honestly report that the only allergies I apparently had were to doctors and hospitals. Things seem to have changed when I had three children of my own, and then sometime later, a fourth. Then it got to the point where the doctors and nurses in various emergency awards throughout the central Plains knew me by name, greeted me at ER doors with a cheery "Hi, Rog. Which kid is it this time?" They kept spare copies of our insurance papers filled out and on file, knowing that it would only be a matter of days before I was back with another bloodied or vomiting child. I knew things were getting out of hand when I drove into the emergency room parking lot at our local hospital with yet another household casualty and found they had painted my name in one of the reserved parking slots. Eventually I requested that they consider using embroidery thread for my children's wounds and perhaps use a nice floral stitch when closing injuries that would show when they grew up. If they ever got as far as growing up.

Then I assisted in the delivery of my fourth child. The first and third were born at an ancient, more primitive time when giving birth was something women did and which men were mercifully spared so they could be out of the cave somewhere defending the campfires against dinosaurs and Cro-Magnons; the second came to us the way children should come into families a lot more often... by adoption. I'll never understand why procreation is celebrated as some sort of special event even though cats, camels, kangaroos, and amoebas do pretty much the same thing. Anyway, I was mostly present...there were black out moments...at the birth of my fourth child and first grandchild. After those two times I discovered I had somehow developed a third allergy...first doctors, then hospitals, and now babies.

A high school basketball coach once said to me, "Welsch, what you lack in coordination, you make up in clumsiness" and I couldn't think of a single comeback with which to contradict him. So, for my first 50 years of life or so I occasionally fell out of a tree, stabbed myself with a baseball bat, hit myself on the back of the head with a hammer, suffered a torn ligament trying to undo a bra clasp, got my foot run over by a car...which I was driving at the time, dropped hot welding spatter into the top of my boots in my shop, fell off a tractor, that kind of thing. But by and large even by the time I reached the age of fifty, I could honestly say I had led pretty much an injury, disease, and disaster free life. I remember distinctly once having a thoughtful moment when I said to myself, "Self, this old body of yours, for all its disproportion (my legs are so short, I am the same height sitting down as I am standing up) has served you well." Through the years, while checking inventory of my health history, I have returned again and again to a hot August day in 19-aught-and 75 when I was working at dismantling a century-old log house. Without major injuries (already a miracle of enormous proportions) friends and I had lowered, moved, and transported the immensely heavy oak and walnut wall logs. As we salvaged what we could, we threw all the shattered remnants no longer useable into the empty basement of the house…splintered roofing, torn tin flashing, boards spiked with ancient rusty nails, bent iron, and broken glass. The abandoned basement where that house had stood was now a hellish pit of sharp, pointed, threatening weapons.

Our next chore was to salvage what we could of the house's rough basement foundation stones, irregular, glacial granite blocks weighing 50 to a hundred pounds. I did this by standing on an old sewer pipe fastened to the inside of the basement wall and heaving the rocks enough to throw them…or more accurately, roll them off the basement wall and out onto the ground outside the basement where we could then roll and load them onto a trailer for transport to the new site for the house. So there I was, filthy from a day's hard labor heaving rocks and logs, my boot toes clinging to the round, soil pipe on the basement wall, facing outward, my back to the basement pit full of razor-sharp, spear-pointed, dirty, rusty, ugly wreckage.

I grunted, growled, and lifted to my naked chest a gigantic granite boulder and muscled it up and out of the basement…almost. The sewer pipe tore loose from the wall while the boulder was still in my arms and on my chest and I fell backwards, with that boulder still in my arms, out onto that mountain of trash under me. My friends working with me on the project pretty much gave up and weren't even sure they should bother to approach the rim of the pit and look down at whatever might be left of me. I rolled the rock off my chest. I struggled to my feet in the waist-deep wreckage and found…I didn't have a scratch. No cuts, nothing broken, not so much as a bruise, not so much as an abrasion, not a drop of blood anywhere on what I was pretty sure when I was in mid-launch would be my corpse. Or pieces of it.

And that's pretty much how life had gone for me to that point…I seemed immune to injury and illness.

The gods heard my expression of contentment and promptly cancelled my warrantees and started the count-down clock on my working parts. In short, old age set in and I started immediately to go to hell in a hand basket. And now it's one thing after another. "Who is my appointment with today? Dentist? Oncologist? Optometrist? Audiologist? Cardiologist? Burn specialist? Osteologist? Geologist? Paleontologist? Buttologist? Wienieologist? Maybe a surprise visit from the EMTs?" It's always something. I now have my magazine subscriptions addressed to various doctors' waiting rooms so I can hope to have something new to read while I wait for my appointment. (A doctor's time is <u>very</u> valuable, you know. Yours of course is not.)

Well, there are many ways we can deal with these inevitabilities…piss and moan, avoid and die, or what the heck, do what you can to accept the inevitable and adopt the Nebraska State Motto as your own watchword: "It Could Be Worse." That's what I do. And that's what this book is about. I hope you find some comfort and humor in these pages and in my discomforts. I've done well writing books about tractor repair and restoration along these lines. Instead of offering up expert opinion, knowing I am anything but an expert, I have instead narrated my foibles, mistakes, and idiocies, thus 1) giving other tractor mechanics some guidelines in what <u>not</u> to do but even more importantly 2) demonstrating that, oh hell, they're not the first to do something stupid in their shop, and 3) I survived and so can they.

Here's to you and your own good health...or at least health that could be worse, after all. And try to think of something smart to say to that receptionist or the doctor him or herself when he or she smiles and says, "Good morning! How are you?" when it should be pretty damned obvious to anyone—and especially these people—that if it were a good morning, and if you were just hunkydamndory you wouldn't be standing there in front of them in a hospital gown with your butt hanging out in the breeze.

# GOLDEN YEARS MY ASS...

My friend Fred Haines pretty much defined the issue for me in a letter I got from him a few days ago. Someone in a welding shop said to him, "Hmmmph…'Golden Years'… The only golden thing about 'the Golden Years' is what's in the specimen cup." Another old friend, Bud Briggs, notes that they are not so much the Golden Years as they are the scrap-iron years. Or maybe the Leaden Years, since it seems that as the years pass, more and more the iron in your blood turns to lead in your rear end.

Okay, now that I've established that it's not easy getting old, I still have to admit that it's considerably better than not getting old. So with that contradiction in mind, I am going to tell you about my, ahem, "Golden Years" with a grumpiness befitting the reality that the process certainly is no lark but also with the laughter than only comes with something that is understood to be inevitable. After all, just like sex, what could be funnier than the processes involved in becoming a Geezer, even if you're the one doing the becoming? If you're over 60—and I presume you are or you wouldn't be reading this—look in a mirror. See? Hilarious! My wife Linda, aside from being our resident wit, is an accomplished artist. She was once asked if she had ever considered doing a full-length nude portrait of me; she responded, "I thought about it...but I don't have enough pink paint. [Dramatic pause...] Or wrinkled paper."

There are even joys that come along with the territory of Geezerdom: for example, old age is what is referred to by geezers like me as an NCZ (No Crapola Zone). There's just no time for baloney, smart alecks, nuisances, annoyances, idiots, and bores when you're over 60. That doesn't mean you have to be rude to nice people but it sure as billy hell gives you permission to tell rude people what you think of them. As my old buddy Mick says, "What are they going to do about it? Take away your birthday?!"

Getting old is not an incurable problem but the cure, like so many of geriatric afflictions, is worse than the problem. But it can be better, and it can be worse. A lot of how you feel about ageing depends on who is around you. I used to be a university professor, for example. On one hand, that can be an invigorating context because you need to keep thinking and you are constantly dealing with young people. On the other hand, it can be an exhausting and frustrating context because...well, because you need to keep thinking and you are constantly dealing with young people. Every year I would stand in front of my classes on the first day of the semester and every year I was one year older, and my students were still each and every one of them somewhere between 17 and 22 years of age. Every year, me one year older...each year, every single one of them the very same age. That gets to be annoying after a while.

Of course not all of you are in a situation like mine. Nonetheless, even if you are a welder or cook, you are trapped in a world where you get older and everyone around you seems to get younger. Inevitably you are, for example, trapped between your parents and your children. You watch your parents get older and in them see what you will become; you look at your children so much younger than you, and remember what you were. There are only a few escape routes from that generational trap, none of them good. Note my brief comment in the Introduction: the cosmetic approach to regaining lost youth is way too visible to be convincing. If anything, it emphasis ageing, and not <u>just</u> ageing but agonized ageing. Plastic surgery fools only the person who has it done. It is, briefly, exactly that…plastic. When a tired, worn-out star appears on television after restoration work, what does he or she think people see and think? How wonderful that person now looks? That the illusion was the ageing and not the repair work? Never. The reaction is at best shock…or likely as not, hilarity. Maybe even contempt: "Who does that idiot think he is fooling?" Obviously—no one.

If you are at all like me, you experience something like one of your children getting married, you think of how old your own parents were when you got married. And you remember how old they seemed then. And you imagine that to your children you must look exactly as old. Yikes! You have become the very geezers you thought your parents were!

My wife Linda is almost 20 years younger than I am. I have children well into their 40s from an earlier marriage, and a daughter in her late 20s. That should keep you young, everyone says. They said that when I was almost 50 years old and Daughter Antonia was three or four: "What a cute little thing! I'll bet she keeps you young!" And I wanted to scream, "Are you out of your damned mind, you idiot?! She keeps me young like trying to ride a mountain lion would keep me young. And it'll be fifteen more years before I can get a decent night's sleep now, so take your 'I'll bet she keeps you young' and trade it in for a toddler of your own!" Of course I wasn't altogether right in my rude ranting: I didn't get off that easy. It's now been 30 years and I still haven't had a decent night's sleep.

Nothing reminds me more brutally of my deepening Geezerhood than our beautiful, vibrant daughter Antonia. All I have to do is look at her and I feel old. All I have to do is say something hopelessly out of date and she will remind me what a geezer I am. She sits here with her Magniflox Hypermodemglo Imagophone that takes photos, tracks satellites, makes airline and hotel reservations, mixes daiquiris, and tunes a guitar, and I innocently ask, "What's that?" And she laughs. Our old bag phone that looks for all the world like a two-suit piece of travel luggage used to send her rolling to the floor in laughter. When it wore out, I asked her what she thought we should do with it and she suggested we donate it to the Smithsonian.

Of course I compounded my own personal ageing situation 25 years ago when I married a woman so much younger than I was. Once again there were the usual comments along the line of "I'll bet that young bride of yours really keeps you young," but the real text was to be found in the sly comments delivered with a sharp jab of an elbow from old-timers who seemed to know all too well that what seemed like an old man's dream might have its downside too: We had been married only a year or so when an elderly veteran commented that we reminded him of the old farmer who married his young hired girl. "Honey, if you ever feel like you want some loving while I'm out in the fields," the Geezer said with a meaningful smile, "Just fire the shotgun and I'll come running." Sadly, the old gent died two weeks into pheasant season.

The jokes abounded in our small town when I first introduced my young bride to my older contemporaries… "A 60-year-old guy tells his 40-year-old wife he's going to trade her in for two 20s, to which she replies, 'And I'll trade you in for two 30s…and 20 goes into 30 a lot more times than 30 goes into 20." And as usual, Linda with her brilliant sense of humor did her part to encourage them. We were in the tavern during one of her first visits to my natural habitat and of course all my buddies started ribbing her…just like they would me. "Hey, Rog, what happened to all those other women you used to bring out here?" "Hey, Rog, is this the one you were telling us about who is so great in bed?" "Rog, whatever happened to that girl you used to date with the huge boobs?"

Now, Linda is a quiet, timid, even shy woman. She never curses, ever. She is gently spoken and pretty sensitive. So I began to worry about how much of this punishment she was going to be able to handle. And I thought I'd say something smart-ass to take my friends' attention away from her and turn it back on me. So I said, "Yep, on April 25th [the projected day for our wedding] there are going to be a lot of disappointed women in Nebraska." And without missing a beat, Linda said…still very quietly and to no one in particular, "I just hope I'm not one of them." And from that moment on, Linda was just another one of the boys. They loved her like a sister and knew that when they needed someone with a sharp punchline to finish off ol' Rog, they could count on her and her wit to do the job.

Probably the most stunning blast of reality about my situation as an older gent with a young bride came to me from my own father. A couple years after we were married, I broke the news to my elderly parents that Linda and I were about to have a baby. Now, understand that I already had grown children; in fact, one of my daughters was already due to have a baby of her own, and as it turned out my first grandchild arrived on the scene exactly three days before my next daughter. So, if my parents were already less than happy about me having the first divorce in the entire history of our family since the time of Noah, and had their doubts about me getting married again, the notion of me having another child at my age was met with considerable… well… considerable skepticism.

After I made my announcement there was a long silence, and then my father, ever the storyteller, said, "Rog, let me tell you a story. There was once an old man out walking in the woods. And he saw a bear. So he raised his cane, pointed it at the bear, and yelled 'BANG!' At the very same instant there was a young man, walking through the woods. He saw the bear too, so he raised his rifle and shot that bear dead. And to this day, the old man thinks he killed the bear with his cane."

There may be advantages to taking on a younger wife but respect may not be one of them.

With a younger wife, I also have younger in-laws. My father-in-law Jake is only a few years older than I am, and my mother-in-law Sally is just a touch older. In fact, I reassured Jake that if things don't work out with me and Linda, I might be interested in taking Sally off his hands. He doesn't seem any more enthusiastic about that idea than he is when I call him "Dad."

Part of the problem is that unlike most cultures around the world, we European-Americans don't have a set of clear milestones to tell us when we've reached a new stage of life. Most societies have set rituals that announce "Now I am an adult" or "Now I am an elder." My parents had church confirmations. Some friends have had bar mitzvahs and bat mitzvahs. Some African tribes declared a boy a man when he had killed a lion and some Native American tribes a youth was a warrior when he had scored a coup against an enemy or killed a bear. We all used to have that sort of milestone system in our societies…Rites of Passage they are called, but not any more. Actually it's not that we don't have any landmarks to make it clear where we stand in the course of our life; we have way too many. It's like a highway with hundreds of mile markers along the roadside, each telling you that you are either almost where you're going or that you went past it many miles ago. Do you become an adult when you graduate from high school? Or maybe from college? Or when you leave home…or get married? Women have it slightly easier than we men: their maturation is indicated around the world when they have their first period, or when their first child is born. But when are men really <u>men</u>? When they enter the military? When they have to pay adult prices to get into a movie…or when they are admitted to an adult film? Is a driver's license proof of maturity? Or maybe the right to buy alcohol? The first time one has sex? You know—like with someone else.

It's not any easier to know when you transited those times when you are still eligible for mid-life crises and arrived at the relative stability and security of those hahahahaha Golden Years. Again, women have an edge with physical signposts like menopause's hot flashes, night sweats, and disinclination to…well…disinclination to. The very morning of writing these words however I found my confidence in the assertion of the previous sentence shaken. Linda headed toward the bathroom with a small box and said she was going to take a self-test to verify her suspicions that she was indeed entering menopause. She came down the stairs with a glum look on her face and declared that the test showed negative results. "I'm not having menopause," she grumped. "That means it's just my personality! I'm just naturally bitchy! And now I <u>am</u> grumpy."

How does a man know when he has indeed reached the status of senior partner? A man's first prostate exam seems a bit early in the game, although that is a memorable landmark for most of us, and something of a surprise if you don't know exactly what is about to happen after the doctor has you drop your pants and bend over.

Is seniority achieved with that first membership invitation to join the AARP arrives in the mail? When I got mine at the age of about 50, I thought it was so funny, I showed it to my mother. She didn't think it was funny at all. Is Geezerhood conferred upon the arrival of that first Social Security check? If so, there may be some people who are going to be forever young if some greedy politicians have their way! (Like John McCain. Yes, that rich bastard who married into his wealth and has so many homes he can't count them, collects—and cashes—his Social Security checks!) Is it the age where you get a free fishing license, or a seniors discount at McDonald's? Is it maybe when you can no longer pass the drivers license test, or when you get your first hearing aid? How about when they throw a retirement party for you? I haven't had a real job for 30 years now, and if you don't have a job, you can't retire. No weekends off, no vacations... unemployment is not an easy life. Have you finally crossed the line into your Hahahahaha Golden Years when all your children finally move out of the house? Or perhaps when they finally all move back in? Nowhere is it written at what point when one's Geezerhood becomes official.

Do you have a right to the title of "elder" when your first grandchild is born? That happened to me when I was only 47 and I was only half way through my first midlife crises, so that doesn't seem a good gauge, although I do recall Linda saying she didn't mind sleeping with a man 47 years old but she sure didn't find much pleasure in her bed partner being a grandfather.

In fact, any sort of bedtime associations may not be good points of reference. On the morning of Linda's 37th birthday I announced…thinking it would please her enormously…that she was now the oldest woman I had ever slept with. Curiously, she didn't say much to me the rest of that entire day. Or week.

I imagine it must have been for her like that unpleasant moment for a man when it is made clear to him by some young lady, or perhaps several, that he is no longer dangerous. Like, "Hey, mister, would you help me tie the strings of my swimming suit top? I can't really ask any of these young men because they just act like it's an invitation to make smart remarks or start exploring, if you know what I mean. But I can trust you. You should be okay…after all, you're an old guy. What harm could you do?" Or, "Sir, would you mind putting some of this sun lotion on my back. You're the only person around here who looks safe." Or how about, "Hey, Gramps, why don't you take my seat? You are looked pretty peaked and we have a long ways yet to go. Mind if my girlfriend sits on your lap the rest of the way?"

That hurts. Or it would hurt if it had ever happened to me. I haven't reached that point yet. I'm pretty sure women still see me as a virile earthquake. Sort of. It's just that I haven't been to the beach or ridden on a bus in a long time. And yet there is always some female spoilsport ready to puncture the geezerly balloon and remind an old man that…that…that, well, that he is an old man. In keeping with a challenging pace set for me by my father, whenever I am in a doctor's care and have a chance to flirt with a nurse, I do. It doesn't matter what she looks like; for some reason my father, and now I, feel the intimacy inherent in health care pretty much requires us to say something suggestive. But these days I find that the new generation of nurses don't understand the importance of such stimulation to us ancients: the usual response I get these days is, "Oh Mr. Welsch, you're so cute. You remind me of my grandpa." Terrific. Or a communication from an attractive young woman I thought I was flirting with who addressed her next note to me, "Dear Uncle Roger…."

It happened to me just the other day so I have a painfully precise example for you. I was arranging for a photo shoot with a young, attractive, divorced female photographer and we were considering places to pose me in a natural, weedy setting. (The book is about edible wild foods.) With something of a leer, I suppose, I said, "Aren't you just a little nervous about going into the weeds under the bridge with me?" Heh heh heh heh heh… "No," she said blithely. "I'll bring some bug spray."

Jeez.

Even if we are no longer "dangerous," we like to think we are. An elderly gent just visited us from Denmark and was outraged that security officers had waved him on through because they took one look at him and presumed he certainly was no threat to national security. The kindest thing a young woman or security agent can do for those of us who are in our Hahahahaha Golden Years is to at least act as if we are sexual predators ready to spring at the slightest hint of an invitation. And the very worst thing a young woman can do is make it clear that she considers us perfectly harmless. While it may be something of an insult to be considered someone of suspicion and danger, even worse is to be seen as someone who presents not the slightest threat. Unless… unless there is a way to use that very attitude to indulge yourself in whatever motivations…if you catch my drift…you have left, and thus prove that there is still something of a fire in the hearth even though there is snow on the roof.

Among the many things I have developed over the years to ease the way into and within the Hahahahaha Golden Years is my copyrighted HOG card…Harmless Old Geezer card.

## HARMLESS OLD GEEZER CARD

| | | | | | | | | | | |
|---|---|---|---|---|---|---|---|---|---|---|
| 1 | The bearer is certified to be harmless. His | | | | | | | | | 31 |
| 2 | deteriorating physical condition and advanced | | | | | | | | | 30 |
| 3 | age entitle him in accordance with the United | | | | | | | | | 29 |
| 4 | States Constitution to one (1) transgression per | | | | | | | | | 28 |
| 5 | day of A) sexual harassment, B) swinish | | | | | | | | | 27 |
| 6 | chauvinism, or C) infantile insensitivity. If you | | | | | | | | | 26 |
| 7 | should be a victim of his misbehavior, check or | | | | | | | | | 25 |
| 8 | punch his card and send the old coot on his way | | | | | | | | | 24 |
| 9 | or return him to (home address): | | | | | | | | | 23 |
| 10 | 11 | 12 | 13 | 14 | 15 | 16 | 17 | 18 | 19 | 20 | 21 | 22 |

I believe one of these cards should be issued to every senior male along with his first Social Security check. Now, don't get me wrong: I don't want drooling old goats stumbling through the streets way too fast for the limitations of their walkers, violating every rule of civilized behavior. But I do feel that a certain amount of latitude should be allowed those of us who

1. offer precious little threat to younger members of the opposite sex since we sometimes don't even have the hand- to-eye coordination to bring thumb to forefinger for a respectable pinch on the rear end of the nurse pushing our wheelchair, even in the confines of an elevator where she doesn't after all leave a lot of wiggle room…as it were;

2. have endured a long life of repression and now that we have the excuse of diminished mental faculty should have at least some compensation for our reduced capabilities;

3. now that we also have other, well, er, reduced physical abilities, if you catch my drift, and are relatively ineffective in the most dramatic of human relations, should at least be given the chance to enjoy what little physical pleasures are available to us.

The Harmless Old Geezer card makes it clear, even to the bearer but more importantly to the recipient of the geezer's attention that there are limits. A Harmless Old Geezer card allows after all only one tabu violation per day. After each anti-social excess, the geezer's card is punched and he is through for that day and can spend the rest of the daylight hours contemplating whatever joy he has derived from his brief moment of libidinous excess.

I have shown this card to quite a few people for evaluation, including not a few women. I have been surprised that they consistently seem to misunderstand its intent. This is <u>not</u> some kind of permit to insult or abuse the opposite sex. If anything, it is an explicit limitation on improprieties.

In fact, I like to think of the attention it permits to be something of a compliment. Imagine that you are a lovely young woman walking along minding your own business and you see an elderly gentleman sitting on a park bench in the sun. He says "Good morning" and being courteous, you smile and return his greeting. Then he says "Excuse me, young lady, but would you mind picking up my book that I dropped over here?" You bend over to pick up the book for him and WHOOPS! Man, that old coot's hands sure are cold!

I suppose you could consider this behavior a violation of common civility and slap his face, but the old goat smiles sweetly and hands you his Harmless Old Geezer card, maybe even offers some sort of lame excuse or apology, and asks you to punch his card since he has now used up his day's allowance of social violations.

First, no harm has actually been done, right? And besides, his card says he is elderly and harmless and gets one such social violation per day. But now, think of this: he has one chance a day to remember his lusty past, one opportunity in each 24-hour period to indulge what's left of his vigor…and today he has elected to spend that one shot of social license on you. He had one free opportunity to express his waning vitality to one woman, and…he chose to spend that one credit on…you! He is in this way complimenting you exclusively today, saying in a way that he cannot repeat for the next 24 hours that you are indeed something special and have brought a ray of sunshine into his life today that excels all others. I think any consideration at all should make it clear that you have just received an enormous compliment, one of the most supreme kind, a sort dealt out very cautiously. I think all but the coldest heart would suggest that instead of a slap, a kind pat on the old man's hoary head, a sweet smile, and maybe a comment like "Why, for shame, you naughty boy, you! If you were thirty years younger...okay, even twenty years older...I might consider asking you back to my apartment for a drink or two, but no, I can't let my baser instincts lead me astray just because you're so cute, you naughty old goat. Here's your card, I checked it and marked it with a little heart symbol, and there's your book. Now, be nice or I'll call the police and tell them there's a naughty, naughty fanny grabber on the loose in the park. Oh, what the heck—go ahead and help yourself to one more little pat, but no pinching, you old rascal." And now...just look at the smile on that old gent's face. Doesn't it say something in the Bible about honoring the elders? I know there are cases where I sure would be honored to be excused for one pat, one pinch, one grope, one gentle goose, one feelie, one...whatever.

Everyone would come out of a transaction like that feeling better. The young lady has been supremely complimented with what is after all a pretty much harmless bit of attention, and one of society's generally ignored Elders has been found a wonderful gift of cheer and a flood of memories that pour forth from even the gentlest pat on a young lady's bottom. Or something.

Just as I caution that we old people have to be a good deal more sensible about things like driving because our reactions slow, our hearing and eye sight fade, and...well, we just don't function as well as we once did. Again, a story makes my point. A senior was moseying down a street one evening and paused to catch his breath. He greeted a young man also standing on the corner and watched him as he trolled for the attention of some young ladies passing by the corner. He would stand there coolly and as the woman approached him he said, "Tickle your ass with a feather…" If the woman reacted negatively and asked him what he had said to her, he would quickly "correct" himself by saying, "I said, 'Typical Nebraska weather…'"

So the old gent thought he would try it for himself, not having had much luck generating any friendly attention for a long time. So he stood there on the corner too and waited for a pretty woman to pass by, blurting out, "Jam a feather up your rear." Of course the woman was outraged and turned to the old man in a fury and asking him what the heck it was that he had said. He stuttered a moment and corrected himself, "Uuuuh, sure looks like rain."

I'm sure you've already noticed but I should probably make the obvious even more so: to my mind the term "Geezer" is gender specific. For one thing, I am a man, and always have been, and have been for quite a while now. I am confident in my maleness…Linda calls it "terminal manhood"…and there's not much I could do in honesty to deny it. But I think geezerliness is a male genetic factor and not just a matter of interpretation. For one thing, women don't get old. Or at least any man who has learned anything at all as he has aged knows for damn sure that he better not suggest anything to that effect. In fact, a sign of the well-matured and trained geezer is that he shouldn't even notice that a woman is anything over 39 years of age, ever. So, this book is about GEEZERS… which is to say redundantly, MALE geezers.

God help the idiot who writes a book for geezerettes. It won't be me, and that's for sure.

Please note too that while I generally favor the terms "Geezer" or "Coot," there are other equally venerated and honorific terms for the condition, e.g.,

Codger
Old-timer
Old settler
Veteran
Artifact

Dinosaur
Oldster
SC (Senior Citizen)
AARPer
Neanderthal
Old goat
Fuddyduddy
Old dog
Yudzer (my father's German term)
Fossil
(Old) Fogy
Reprobate
Over-the-Hiller
Pensioner
Et al.

The consequences of growing old may not even be a matter of being unwilling to admit what has become of us—or is in the process of becoming of us; we may actually not <u>know</u> yet that we have reached the threshold of harmlessness. I was once at a ritual meeting with some of my Native American family and friends and after a long session that had gone on through the night from sunset to dawn we were nearing the end of our vigil. One of the younger participants in our gathering needed to speak to the gathering but in the custom of Native peoples, if he wanted to speak before the elders, he would have to get the permission of the elders. He respectfully therefore asked the permission of the elder in the group to speak. There was a long silence as we waited for that permission to be granted. I sat as patiently as I could, head down, eyes closed, exhausted from the demands of a long night of sitting up on the ground, an exercise that would tire a man half or a third my age, hoping the elder in attendance, whoever he might be, would be quick with his response. Still no permission was forthcoming.

The painful silence continued. Finally, I looked up and around the circle hoping to see some sign that the elder of the group would at long last grant this man the permission to speak. And I saw...all eyes on <u>me</u>! Good grief! Everyone saw my surprise...I couldn't hide it!...and there was general laughter because everyone realized that I had just figured out what they all already knew--<u>I</u> was the elder at this gathering! Age can do that...sneak up on you when you're not paying any attention. You may be old at this very moment and not even know it! Check your drivers license. What does it say under the category "STATUS." If it says "Geezer," you may want to give that some thought.

It's important to consider this matter because even if you don't, sooner or later it's going to be brought to your attention. Believe me, you can't avoid Geezerhood simply by ignoring it. I once rushed Linda to the emergency ward for an eye injury, for example. We checked in and found we were the only ones in the waiting room. The attending physician came out to talk with Linda and...wow!...this woman (the doctor, that is!) was movie star gorgeous. I looked around to see if maybe a camera was rolling somewhere to catch our surprise at the stunning attractiveness of this doctor, or maybe if we hadn't stumbled onto a film set accidentally. She talked briefly with Linda...and gave me a look that spoke volumes. She was a doctor so she wasn't some vacant-headed teenager, but neither was she very old...maybe 35. She was obviously incredibly well conditioned...trim, groomed, composed, strong-- a figure that was impressive even in her scrubs. She was stunning in her confidence and glowing beauty. Even women like this, I found from ample experience during a long bachelorhood between marriages, find a mature man like me attractive...maybe it's our sophistication, a promise of skills learned over the years...I don't know, but this woman, despite her own charms, obviously saw that something special in me. She began to lead Linda away to an examining room and then paused, turned seductively to me, her eyes meeting mine. She turned back to Linda and said, "And if you like, your father can come along with you...."

Hmmmm.... Well.... Actually, now that I think about it, the woman wasn't nearly as attractive as I first thought. In fact she was a little dumpy and disheveled. Her features showed just a hint of coarseness and her voice was like a knife blade on glass. Frankly, I'd bet now that she was a lesbian. In fact I'm pretty sure of it.

Speaking of doctors...and believe me, we will be speaking of doctors since 98% of what any Geezer talks about on a daily basis focuses on medical conditions, conversations amounting to what are called by the callow young "organ recitals."

Another thing you are going to have to get used to during your dotage are not just female doctors, not just attractive doctors, but doctors who are so young you may, as I recently did, ask to see a drivers license so if they had to make it to the hospital quickly to repair your spleen, they wouldn't have to resort to a Big Wheel trike or skateboard for transportation. It's even worse when these doctor-children fall into the category of Children Whose Parents Apparently Never Thought They Would Amount to Anything. Think about it—if you think your child is going to be anything at all...or for that matter even grow up to be an adult...would you name him Mikalee, JayObob, or Shaksupremepoo? Or dub her Krystal, Sherilee, Shacquerbo, LaWondra, or Coddee? How about Brie, Camembert, or Cheddar? Amberglow or Sweetsiepie? Of course you wouldn't. Most people invest more time in thinking up names for their boats than they do their children. People who inflict names like the above on their infant are absolutely sure the kid will never be President of the United States, and that's for damn sure. People want their boats to be impressive, respected, or even intimidating. Way too many people figure their children will be forever children, cute and loveable even though 97% of them have left that stage by the time they reach four or five, if in fact they were ever anything but ugly little hellions to begin with.

Some parents apparently never imagine that their children will be a Congressman, Supreme Court justice, business CEO ...or a doctor. Doctors should have names like John, William,

Don, Robert, Albert, Jacob, or Carl. Doctors should not have names like Pinky, Elvis, Bambi, Tiffany, Toby, Rainbo, Moonbeam, Kelsee, Cammie, Tara, Deena, Ashley, Salamee, Chelsee, Amye, Brittanie, Tammy, Makaylala, Heatherfeather, or anything else that is also the name of a coldcut or imported cheese. When you run into a doctor who insists that you call him "Doctor White," "Doctor Smith," or "Doctor Schmeckenberger," or who is listed in the telephone book as "S. B. White," "R. J. Smith," or "K. Schmeckenberger," you can just about bet that his or her first name is Stacee, Rowdy, Bambi, Cutsy, Provolone, Chastonia, or Kryztalle.

In fact, you can almost tell a geezer from a non-geezer from his name. Bob, George, Roger = Geezer; Klay, Hootie, Jamie, Dakota, = punk-ass kid. Not long ago there was a letter in our newspaper from a woman who complained that her child's name had been misspelled in a report about a baseball game in which he had scored the winning run. His name, she huffed, is MaiKell. I think the editor apologized but if he'd had any backbone at all…that is, if he were a Geezer no longer willing to put up with crapola…he would point out that she was the one who had misspelled the kid's name. It's Michael. M-I-C-H-A-E-L. And then I'd make her write it over and over again until she got it right. Believe me, it wouldn't be long before the paper would have been publishing a letter of profound gratitude from the poor wretch of a kid who had had this monstrosity of a moniker inflicted on him by a cruel, cruel parent. I just looked in our local paper and in one single article about school activities there are children named Kati, Jami, Sami, Palli, Pooki, Cootie, and Cali. Parents who do something like this to their children should be sent to prison without a trial…for their own protection, because sooner or later Kati, Jami, Sami, Palli, Pooki, Cootie, and Cali are going to kill them. And any judge with a sense of justice will call those murders justifiable.

(Also, note the sarcastic and excessive indignation of the preceding jeremiad. A rant like this is a sure sign of a Geezer. It takes practice but you'll get the hang of it eventually. Practice makes perfect. There is a reason geezers are sometimes described as "garrulous," a fancy word meaning "yells at clouds.")

An inevitable consequence of getting old is that all your friends are getting old too. And inevitably too many of them (you'll come to hope <u>all</u> of them!) die before you do. It's like the old story of the man who wisely concludes that what's important is not so much out-running the grizzly bear that invades the company picnic as it is out-running just one other person being chased by that same bear. At any rate, there is always of course some chance that a friend or relative will die when you are still young; but when you are old, your friends and relatives drop around you like flies when the bug spray goes to work. It gets to be downright depressing, and no one seems to want to help.

And then you go to the funerals. In fact, when you're a Geezer, it seems like every week you go to the funerals. You start to check the obituaries in the newspaper just to make sure you're not listed as one of the dearly and newly departed. But as my old pal Eric once wisely told me, "Thing is, you pretty much have to go to your friends' funerals because if you don't go to theirs, they're not going to be going to yours."

No, you might just as well go ahead and admit it…you're getting old. Don't mince words. Don't pussyfoot around with "ageing," "senior years," "geriatric," "getting on in years," or that accursed irony "The Hahahahaha Golden Years." Nope, you're getting just plain, flat-out <u>old</u>. I had no more than turned 65 when one blizzardy winter night the television weatherman said "It's going to be a bitterly cold one tonight, ladies and gentleman, so it just might be a good idea to check on any elderly folks you are concerned about," and without so much as a hesitation for courtesy, Linda turned to me and said, "Well…how <u>are</u> you doing, Rog?"

And just this last week Linda was filling out a renewal subscription form for a news magazine I enjoy and she said to me, "Hey, Rog, how have you been feeling?" "Well, fine, I guess," I said, mystified by her question. "Okay, then…good," she said, and then she checked the box for a two-year renewal, a substantial savings over the one-year option.

The main thing, the bottom line, is to carpe the damn diem. If you don't grab for all the advantages...the few advantages... Geezerhood carries with it, you can pretty much kiss them goodbye because no one these days is going to go out of his or her way to make sure you get them. There are still societies in this world where age is seen as an asset and virtue, a sure sign of wisdom from making a lot of mistakes along the way, if nothing else. But not here in the good ol' US&A. Here, you're a pain in the ass when you're old, so why not make sure you are a productive pain in the ass? Or at least a memorable pain in the ass?

Celebrate your age. Don't try to hide it. Forget the Grecian Formula nonsense, and cosmetic surgery, pills to make you feel young, or look young, or poop young... Be old and proud. Seize the day! Flaunt your Geezerhood! Celebrate Geezerdom! To the barricades! A bas la jeunesse! Assert the privilege seniority! Insist on your rights as a senior!

That's what I intend to do. Right after my nap. And my daily dose of prune juice. And a bowl of bran flakes.

# MAINTENANCE AND REPAIRS...

This book is about the medical complications of getting old. Which is the greater part of getting old. In fact, now that I think about it, there's not much more to getting old than medical concerns. Forget an "annual check-up." Linda used to remind me every couple years about getting a medical check-up, "just in case." Some times a couple years went by without us remembering the routine. No big deal. The results of the exams were always the same: "Rog, you could afford to lose some weight. Your blood pressure is a little high. Drop your pants. Bend over. Spread your legs." Blahblahblahblahblah...

Now just about the only thing Linda and I do together any more is go to our appointments with doctors. It gets to be as ordinary as the sunrise. You carry your magazines into the waiting room because you know exactly what reading material each doctor has, and you've already seen it all. You read the clinic's magazine collection when they were only six years old and now they are antiques. The receptionists in the dozen or so doctors' offices we frequent now recognize our car as we park, and they greet me with "Hey, Rog...the usual?" just the way barmaids used to.

There is some hazard in regularity of appointment patterns, of course, because even the slowest male eventually figures out when the time is coming for yet another medical unpleasantry and can therefore develop special ways to avoid them. Linda has taken to "stealth appointments," for example: she tells me she is going to the dermatologist to have some nasties removed from the bottom of her foot. Which of course means she won't be able to drive. And she needs me to go along as chauffeur. "Bring a book," she says coyly, further creating a diversion from the plot. We enter the doctor's waiting room, sign in, and I settle down for a nice long read while she prepares herself for female examining room tortures.

I almost never notice however that...hmmm...she really doesn't seem all that anxious. And she is the anxious type. So.... And then the nurse opens the door into the waiting room and says, "Roger, you can come in now." I can't reveal what a big sissy I am in front of all these people and what might be an attractive nurse. Even worse, I can't show what an idiot I am not to have known that I was there for my <u>own</u> appointment, thinking all the while I was there for <u>Linda's</u> visit. I am developing strategies to deal with these drive-by doctor's appointments but I also know it won't do me a bit of good. Linda is always way ahead of me and probably has six or ten other deceptions already plotted out should I ever get clever enough to detect and avoid these.

You know you have reached some kind of geezerly plateau when you no longer care whether the opening is in the front or the back when you put on your hospital gown. After my orientation visit at the local cancer clinic in preparation for a series of radiation treatments (about which more later) I was walking down the clinic hallway in my hospital gown and realized that it had gathered up in the back and I was showing more of my base line than either I or anyone else would prefer to make public. I stopped and considerably flustered tried to get the thing into some position to serve its intended mission. Now, you have to realize that I am six foot two and weigh about 280 pounds and hospital one-size-fits-all gowns are made for someone five foot six tipping the scales at 150 pounds at the most. It didn't help that the attending radiation technologist, a notably attractive woman named Carla , who will show up later in these pages because she is a real attention getter if you catch my drift, was right behind me and instantly realized my embarrassment as I flailed around behind me trying to close the gaping gown that was opening for all the world like the stage curtain at the Roxie.

"I'm trying to maintain my dignity," I sputtered.

With a sweet, kindly, sympathetic but completely frank tone she said, "Roger, it's too late. Your dignity is pretty much a lost virtue today as far as I'm concerned, and believe me, once these treatments start... your dignity and modesty are going to be nothing but a fond memory."

Carla isn't just a radiation technologist...she is also a philosopher. They should have a sign over the door at the Geezer Clinic that says ABANDON DIGNITY ALL YE WHO ENTER HERE. But don't despair. It's like the loss of any kind of dignity. Remember how embarrassed you were the first time in a moment of passion you...well, you know...did...uh...you know...you did you know what? But that eventually turned out pretty well, right? Sometimes dignity gets in the way of what really counts. If you are facing any sort of medical indignity, then you are now about to bump up against the bottom line of this book: Forget false pride and embrace the human condition. You can piss and whine about what you are about to endure in cancer treatment, a hernia operation, or a cardiac catheterization...or you can laugh and find in it what pleasure you can. Hey... so it was embarrassing. Make the best of it. Look at it this way: on this occasion, at the age of 67 I actually flashed my bare bottom at a very pretty woman named Carla. And she didn't scream and run away. Yeah, I know it's her job but when you are over 60, you take your comfort where you can.

Growing accustomed to medical vicissitudes can be discouraging (does one really <u>want</u> to get used to being prodded, poked, probed, and perused?) or simply a matter of course. I prefer to take the latter path. In our household we have come to think of the clink of a spoon in a glass mixing up my daily dose of Citrucel as our Happy Hour—particularly appropriate with poultry or seafood…presumptuous, full-bodied, faint hint of orange, with great nose and body and just a hint of oak. The thrice-daily handful of pills regulating my various irregularities is as colorful and festive as a big bowl of Fruit Loops. When Linda announces it's time for yet another visit to yet another doctor's office, I think of it as a signal of her concern for me and her way of inventing a pretext to see some part of my body unclothed. (Don't bother asking her; I don't think she sees it that way.) Besides, the attending nurse this time may be the fetching Carla over whom we will drool later in these pages.

Our increasingly frequent trips to doctors are the closest thing Linda and I have to a date, after all. We feel perfectly comfortable planning a nice meal after even a scheduled proctologic examination. What's even more clearly a sign of Geezerhood…you know what a proctologic exam is but you still go! As Ted Haines's welder buddy noted, it gets to the point when he sees someone in the auto shop pulling on rubber gloves to work with parts cleaner, he automatically drops his pants and bends over.

That has to be just about the most common and demeaning indignity man has to endure, right up there with what stirrups mean to a woman. I did have just a scintilla of revenge only two weeks ago. I was peddling books at a tractor show not far from here when who should show up but our family doctor. I like Doc Stanton…he's a really good guy, a tractor man, and understanding of both my medical failings, the damage he does to my pride, and my sense of humor…a rare combination. Well, Bill looked over my books, noticed my dog book <u>A Life with Dogs</u> which he had not yet acquired, he bought it, we chatted, and then we said our farewells and he elbowed his way through the modest crowd near my table at the show. Then Satan struck and spoke through my mouth. I yelled after him and over the noise of the crowd, "Hey, Bill! It's really nice to see you for once when you don't have me drop my pants and bend over!" The room went suddenly silent and a hundred eyes slowly turned to look at me...and then Bill. With a look of utter dismay on his face, probably close to what I must look like when he does indeed tell me to drop my pants and bend over, Bill said back...it was so quiet there was no need to yell... "I'm a doctor! I'm a doctor!" Sometimes what goes around does indeed come around.

Twenty-five years ago I didn't know proctology from the doxology. I think the first time I got a glimmer was when I was sitting at the Big Table in my little town's Chew 'n' Chat Café when my old pal Bumps came clomping in. Someone said, "You're late, Bumps. Where've you been?"

"Oh, I was over at Doc Matthews's office getting a proctological exam" Bumps said.

"What the heck is a 'proctological exam?'" asked someone else.

"Well," Bumps sighed, "that's when the doctor tells you to drop your drawers and lean over his little examination table. And then he puts on a rubber glove and tells you to brace yourself, and he puts his right hand on your right shoulder, and his left hand on your left shoulder, and...well...uh...that son of a bitch!"

Which is not to say anything ever gets to be routine when it comes to doctoring and the geezerly. I hate going to a doctor in any event but nothing riles my blood more than when they rile my blood. I don't know if my veins are particularly small, particularly tough, or particularly elusive but I know for a fact that blood-letters who otherwise have no trouble whatsoever in finding and tapping veins at the rate of ten or twenty an hour wind up fishing around for fifteen or twenty minutes with that damn needle trying to find someplace to put a hole in mine. Is it really a good idea to put the needle into the flesh and then fish around for a vein? I'm no phlebotomist (fancy language for "vampire") but I do wonder about this approach to the procedure. A woman was once fishing around in the back of my hand for a gusher, I was turning green and looking for a soft spot on the floor to land on, when Linda, knowing my talent for self-injury, offered up a sensible solution: "Why don't you give him a butter knife and before you know it you'll have all the blood you need."

I dread nothing quite as much as giving a blood sample... although actually "give" isn't quite the word since I surrender such sacrifices only with enormous reluctance. Bleeding is not a problem with me...the sight of blood means nothing. But oh man, a needle.... An Indian princess once recommended to me that instead of going in for flu shots I should just pour myself a generous tot of my favorite bourbon and call it good. As she so poetically phrased it, "A shot in the glass is better than a shot in the ass." Ah, wisdom from the ages....

And that's the moral I want to offer up...there are solutions to these medical problems. A standard geriatric joke tells of the doctor finishing up an examination of his elderly patient and telling him, "When you come back in, Elmer, bring me test specimen of your stool, urine, and ejaculate." "WHAT DID HE SAY?" the geezer yells to his wife, leaving the office with him. "HE SAYS HE NEEDS TO SEE YOUR UNDERWEAR!" the long-suffering wife answers.

If you think that's only a joke, far too unlikely to be anything but a folktale, let me tell you an absolutely true story. A friend of mine hauled his ancient grandfather-in-law into town for a doctor's appointment once and couldn't wait on his return to tell me the story of what had happened. The nurse handed the old gent a specimen cup and told him she would need a sample of his urine and that he should go into the men's room and fill the cup. The doddering old guy sputtered, "What with my hands shaking so bad, there's no way I'm going to be able to hold myself up, get ready to take a leak if you catch my drift, and hold the cup at the same time. Maybe if you could go into the men's room with me and hold the cup...."

Everyone present got a good laugh when the nurse said, "I don't think so! If you're so shaky you're worried about hitting the cup, I'm sure not going to hold it for you!"

"Well," said the geezer, "In that case I'll hold the cup and <u>you</u> do the aiming!"

I vowed on the spot to try line of reasoning that the next time I go in for a check up and Missie Carla Pretty Nurse hands me a specimen cup to fill. And my hands don't even shake.

During my radiation treatments for prostate cancer, my oncologist put me on a drug called FloMax. I asked him what it was designed to do for me and he said, "Well, Rog, it's meant to…uh…encourage…er…well…<u>max</u>…<u>flow</u>." Rarely are medications quite so plainly labeled. Now that I have to get up out of a warm bed two or three times a night to shake hands with the unemployed as the process is sometimes referenced I believe I'm ready for some FloMin.

These days you don't even have to go to a doctor's office to have the medical humiliations of your geezerhood made perfectly apparent to you and everyone around you. I have no idea why, but television is blistered all over with commercials for various geriatric medications. Why do pharmaceutical manufacturers advertise anyway? If their medications work, isn't it pretty much a matter of course that they will be used? And what good does it do to tell <u>me</u> about them, when 1) I don't know what's wrong with me and 2) I don't know what I need to cure it? All the constant television bombardment of geezerly medications does is remind me of everything that's going wrong with me. Loose bowels, stove-up bowels, forgetfulness, aches and pains, hair loss, bad feet, poor eyesight, fungus, bungus, hearing loss… Every night the television commercials during the evening news are like an inventory of the medical complaints I've had since breakfast.

Don't even get me started on the endless commercials for male wick stiffeners! While I do get some comfort from the ads in learning that I'm not the only one who has the problem, I take little comfort in learning that if I take this pill I'll be able to throw a football through a tire swing or, the most common apparent side effect of "male enhancement" potions, Linda and I will take up dancing. What's the deal with all that dancing? This couple takes some blue pills for what the guy in the lab coat calls "erectile dysfunction" and the next thing you know, they're doing the tango. I wasn't all that crazy about dancing when my erector set worked fine, and I'm sure as hell not very enthusiastic about dancing now that it takes me all night to do what I was used to do all night, if you catch my drift. I don't want to dance...don't ask me.

Okay, I've made my point: there may not be a clear set of criteria that must be met before you are securely mired in your seniority. But believe me, you'll know when you are there. The evidence will pile up regardless of whatever resistance you put up. It cannot be stopped or reversed. We all know how funny...often grotesque...people look who try to stop time or turn it back. Whether it's with spackle and paint, plastic surgery, wigs, comb-overs, stucco, prostheses, or simply acting stupid, is anything more obvious than the tired Hollywood has-been who spent too much time in the sun trying to regain youth with reconstructive surgery?! All that kind of stupidity does is to enrich the potential for imagination: "Wow...look at all that plastic surgery! Looks like a lip tuck, wrinkle removal, hair transplants, nose bob, neck ironing, breast trestling.... Can you imagine how old that poor reprobate must be if he/she needs that much work? I would guess maybe 97 years old, huh?" Seen in natural cragginess this rebuilt derelict would be judged to be 63, which is precisely right and much more flattering. Or simply deal with reality?

The question is not so much whether you are going to get older or younger, spend more time or less time with doctors probing your privacy. The real issue is how you are going to deal with it. Are you going to fight it futilely? Try to ignore it at the peril of others and yourself? Use it as an excuse to be a pain in the ass for everyone around you?

I learned my lessons about ageing from my father, Chris Welsch. God knows, he had his share of health problems and as a result was in his geezerhood long before most of us reach that plateau. For example, he was struck by lightning when he was a kid, had a stroke in his old age, lost a finger to a lawnmower, heart attacks…the works. My impression is that all of us think of our parents as eternally old, forever Geezers, but in Dad's case I know for a fact that was in part an accurate assessment because he had some afflictions of the elderly earlier than most of us. He was only 14 years old when he was working as a laborer in the sugar beet fields of western Nebraska and was struck by lightning. He was unconscious for almost a week, was of course badly burned, and came out of his coma deaf for life. At 65 I began to go deaf, the result not of lightning but of a lifetime of rock and roll music, unmufflered tractor engines, two marriages, and three daughters. And I finally came to understand my father better than I ever had in the previous two-thirds of a century. That is, as my own afflictions accumulated, I understood my father (and every other old-timer) even better.

And I grew too to understand how Dad dealt with all his physical problems: he laughed at them. From his tiniest problems to the biggest, he laughed. Never with irony or cruelty, and almost always at himself. And in so doing, he threw his defiance into the face of adversity more surely than if he had screamed his anger at the heavens and thrown rocks at God.

One of my earliest memories was a time when Dad and I were working in our Victory Garden…that term will give you other Geezers some idea of how long ago this story took place…and a bird pooped on Dad's head. I don't know how to describe the situation any more delicately than that. Plop. A bird dropped a load right on my father's head, right in front of me. And it was mulberry season. The enormous blotch on my father's forehead was a purple horror.

I was only six or seven years old and this was my dad. I watched in total dismay as he reached into his back pocket, took out a red kerchief, and slowly carefully wiped the mess out of his hair. I waited for the explosion. The invention of the atomic bomb had yet to be revealed to the world but at that moment that's pretty much what I expected even without knowing that horror yet. But that was when I got my first lesson from Dad in how to deal with the inevitable, unavoidable, or irreversible... Dad wiped the mess from his head, looked up, and said quietly, "For the rich, you sing."

And he went back to his gardening. He never said a word to me about the event, didn't even look to see if I had heard him or appreciated his aplomb. He didn't need to because he wasn't saying it for my benefit, and certainly not for the offensive bird, who was long gone. He delivered his punch line for himself. He could have been angry, or disgusted, or embarrassed but none of those would have done anything whatsoever to change matters. So he laughed. He probably didn't make that line up. I imagine he heard that gag line somewhere else, or read it on a comic postcard somewhere. Doesn't matter. What does count is that 1) he remembered it and 2) had the composure to deliver it when the gods of humor were kind enough to deliver him the softball straight line of a huge dollop of liquid mulberry bird poop splashing on his head.

Fate dealt my father a lifetime of deafness. So what did he do about it? Of course he threw back in gleeful defiance a lifetime of punch lines about...deafness. He came to specialize in jokes about deafness. He wasn't being cruel to the deaf. Hell no! <u>He was after all deaf!</u> It never let up. I don't know where he got all his lines but as the comic line goes, he had a million of 'em.

He told of going to the doctor when his hearing aids no longer seemed to be helping him and of the doctor's surprise when he peered into Dad's ears and found...a suppository. "Chris!" the doctor sputtered. "There's a suppository in here!" whereupon Dad said, "So...<u>that's</u> where my hearing aid went!"

I once found the courage to ask a personal question of my dad, that is, why I was an only child. Dad answered without hesitation, "Because I got a hearing aid." Puzzled, I continued, "Uh, Pop, what would a hearing aid have to do with me being an only child?" He said, "When your mother and I were first married and would go to bed, she'd say, 'Well, Chris, do you want to go to sleep, or what?' and I'd say, 'WHAT?' Then you were born and I got a hearing aid." I no longer had a question about why I was an only child. I wondered instead about the comic genius of my Old Man.

Linda and I, her parents and mine were on our way to a Caribbean cruise and were amusing ourselves in a waiting room in Pittsburgh waiting for the next flight when Dad started telling us about his new hearing aid. He explained that it was at the cutting edge of microtechnology, a miracle of miniaturization and acoustics, a triumph of audiology. Ever the straight man, I asked, "Wow, Dad, what kind is it?" and with perfect timing he checked his watch and said "About ten minutes after two…"

One of his favorite deaf-geezer jokes dealt with a young fellow traveling down the highway somewhere in Nebraska who stops over at a roadside eatery for a piece of pie and a cup of coffee. He sits at the counter beside an elderly couple and strikes up a conversation by asking, "Where you folks from?" to which the aged gent responds, "Oh, we're from up in Sioux Falls." The old lady, obviously deaf, shouts, "WHAT DID HE SAY?" and the old man impatiently answers "HE WANTS TO KNOW WHERE WE'RE FROM AND I TOLD HIM WE'RE FROM SIOUX FALLS!"

"Where you folks headed?" the young man asks. "We're headed down to Kansas City," answers the elder. "WHAT DID HE SAY?" the old lady shouts, and her husband responds, "HE WANTS TO KNOW WHERE WE'RE GOING AND I TOLD HIM WE'RE GOING TO KANSAS CITY!"

"Hmmm, well, I can tell you this," the young man says, "the worst sex I ever had in my life was in Kansas City." The old lady says, "WHAT DID HE SAY?" and the old man shouts back at her "HE SAYS HE KNOWS YOUR SISTER!"

The older you get, the more embarrassing your afflictions become. Take BPPV, or "Benign paroxysmal positional vertigo," a real term. Look it up. Pretty impressive, huh? Well, what it means is that you have had a rock slide in your head. No kidding. Rocks. Breaking loose and slamming around in your head. Small crystals at the base of the filaments in your inner ear break loose, rattle against the filaments, and induce totally disabling vertigo and sock-puking nausea makes you think you're dying but winds up being little more than a verification of your children's diagnoses since their teen years, that you are 1) dizzy and 2) have rocks in your head.

One of the things Dad always recommended, having been deaf all his life, was that we elderly could save a lot of money by not buying expensive hearing aids. He advised, "Just pass a piece of black string over your ears and down the front of your shirt. That way people will assume you are wearing a hearing aid and talk louder."

As Dad grew older and his afflictions multiplied…as they do and will, I can assure you!…he branched out smoothly into stories and punch lines about being old. He delighted especially in embarrassing my mother, who after all was growing old with him. So, he told about the time they went in together for an annual check up, both well into their 80s. The doctor examined Dad and said, "Chris, you seem to be in pretty good condition considering your age. Is there anything that seems to be bothering you in particular?" "Well, yes," Dad reported telling him. "I am a bit concerned that the second time my wife and I have sex I sweat so bad."

The doctor said, "I'm not sure what might cause that but let's do some further tests and I'll see if I can figure it out and get back to you on what the problem might be and how to deal with it."

Then the doctor examined Mom and asked her "Mrs. Welsch, I'm worried about Chris. He says he sweats so bad the second time you folks have sex…"

"Well, the old fool," Dad said Mom sputtered, "The second time we have sex is usually in August!"

While Dad was always in part mitigating the discomfort of ageing for himself, this was also his way of easing whatever sadness the rest of us might feel in seeing the old gent struggling through his dotage. One particularly vivid example of this strategy on his part came when we were sitting around my parents' apartment once talking about their youth and courtship and Mom was telling about how abysmally poor they were when they first met, courted, and married, smack dab in the middle of the Great Depression. Mom told about having to turn over to her step-parents her paycheck from the laundry where she did hard, hot, dirty work and thus going into her and Dad's marriage without a penny to her name. Dad had to pay for her wedding dress...and he had to borrow the money for new socks to be married in. Mom was at the edge of tears when she recalled having to walk from her former home with her step-parents—she had been an orphan since childhood—to her new home with Dad, without a possession or dollar to her name.

It was an uncomfortable moment for us all as we sat there listening to her, resonating with her memories of her pain and embarrassment. I turned to Dad, trying to redirect some of the focused silence in the room, and said to him, "Pop, you weren't exactly a high roller at the time"—he was shoveling coal at a power plant at the time—"so what kind of fortune did <u>you</u> bring to this union?"

"I had $92 in postal savings," he said, "and on the day we were married, I turned it all over to your mother."

"Was she worth the investment?" I tried to joke.

But it was up to Dad to deliver once again the punch line: "Time will tell," he said. "Time will tell." After 65 years of marriage, he was still hedging his bets, holding open his options, weighing the evidence. And what's more important, alleviating pain with laughter. It was his way. "Time will tell." In the last cogent hours of his life he told Mom he loved her, made everyone laugh, and flirted with a nurse. (He was obviously in his last hours. The hospice nurse pressed at his neck and asked him if there was any pain. He said no, there was not. She pressed a finger against his ribs and asked again. No, no pain. She pressed her hand against his abdomen. Pain? No. She pressed in his groin. Did that hurt? "No," he smiled. "In fact...<u>that</u> is starting to feel kinda good.")

That's the way I want to go too. And that's what this book is about. I have had my share of geezer afflictions-- no more than usual, however, and certainly not all I'm going to suffer before I cash in my chips. So there it is. I'm getting old. But I've managed to get through the problems or along with them and I hope my stories will help you get through or along with yours too. Face it: You're going to have plenty of geriatric afflictions. It's inevitable. It is part of life. We sometimes forget that in modern America but it's true.

When Dad was dying a hospice worker came to talk with us about what he was going through and a couple things she said surprised me with their obviousness, bits of clarity I had somehow missed...or ignored...up to that point. She said that what Dad was going through and that we were witnessing was all perfectly normal, a matter of regular course, nothing at all unusual in dying. In fact, she gave us a pamphlet outlining step by step what we could expect as he started on that long, mysterious journey. It is, after all, a process we've had plenty of chance to observe for the last several hundred thousand years. Curiously, it helps us to know what to expect. We do all die, and a lot of us die a natural death. That's why it's called a <u>natural</u> death...because death <u>is</u> natural.

The second thing the hospice worker said that struck me with its frankness and obvious truth was that from the moment of birth, we are all "terminal." Well, uh, yeah...sure. I guess that's true. Even if we don't like to think about it, it's true. If anything in this world is true, that is true. Isn't that what they say, after all? "Death and taxes...." And these days even the second inevitability may be avoidable if you are a rich Republican with accounts in a bank in the Cayman Islands.

I don't want to get all morbid here but this ageing process and its, uh, conclusion is as much a part of life as birth. And perhaps that is the best way to look at it...not with a whimper or a bang but a chuckle. I don't whimper, and I don't bang...at least not as much as I used to. So I've decided it's going to be a chuckle that I'll go off stage with. I hope you won't so much laugh at me as with me. Even if you're not yet old, sooner or later, you will be. As my Old Man would have put it, "Time will tell."

I don't know what becomes of us after we die. Actually, and to be totally honest, neither does anyone else, including and maybe even especially those who insist that they <u>do</u> know. Look at them. Now, aren't they just about the dumbest people you've ever encountered? What is the likelihood of them knowing more about <u>anything</u> than you do? Zero. Take it from me, I don't know what happens when we die. You don't know what happens when we die. No one knows what happens when we die. The change may be dramatic; it may wind up being nothing at all. I once said something to Linda about re-incarnation, the notion of some that we are reborn again and again. In fact, I said, in a previous life, we may even have been an animal. "Or," Linda said in her matter-of-fact tone, "in your case, in <u>this</u> life." God, I love that woman.

A day came when we had to consider putting down, as the phrase goes, our dear old cat Hairball. She was 18 years old, tough as nails, but failing fast. She had lost control of almost everything, made a mess at least once a day in Linda's studio, was barely alive, yet capable of taking care of herself. But Linda was nonetheless reluctant to take the inevitable step of putting her "to sleep." (Why can't American's say words like "die," "death," or "dead?" It's almost like a speech impediment.) Anyway, as I watched this process from afar…I am not the cat person in the household… I mentioned that I was taking some comfort in Linda's reluctance to euthenize this scraggly, troublesome, messy, stinky, battered old soul, since the time was going to come when I was going to be in pretty much the same condition. "And I imagine you will be just as reluctant to have them put <u>me</u> down…" I said confidently.

The pause following that was already way too long, but then she said, "Not really. It will probably depend on the amount of pain being endured." Okay…I guess that makes sense. But again she spoiled the moment: "That would be mine. Not yours…."

# THE HEART OF THE MATTER:

The first really hard lesson I had in my own mortality happened, as it usually does, at a moment when I didn't at all expect it. I was an essayist on CBS News Sunday Morning with my old friend Charles Kuralt, doing occasional stories for that wonderful show on ordinary rural life titled "Postcards from Nebraska." I was in South Sioux City at my favorite hotel in this world, the Marina Inn, in a nice room with a gorgeous view north over the Missouri River toward Sioux City. I had completed a good, successful day's work with my CBS crew…cameraman Isadore Bleckman, soundman Danny Gianneschi, producer E. S. "Bud" Lamoureaux, no longer just colleagues but dear, close friends. We had just finished an excellent dinner with another old friend, Louie LaRose, keeper of the Winnebago Tribe's bison herd, with whom we were going to tape a story the next day. We ate, drank, and laughed, and then went to bed. I was happy, comfortable, content with the day's work and anticipating the next.

I woke up about 2 in the morning, however, feeling very uncomfortable… a bad case of indigestion, I guessed. Small wonder… I had probably eaten too much as usual, probably had a glass or two too much wine, had laughed myself to near exhaustion...all on top of a rigorous day's work. And I was in a strange bed, never the best place for rest. I had increasingly found that eating late in the evening, especially <u>heavy</u> eating, was leaving me uncomfortable through the night...just another symptom of growing old, I figured, probably with some good reason.

I got up and went to the bathroom. I drank some water. I grew increasingly uncomfortable however and clearly was not going back to sleep. The pressure in my torso seemed...well... worse than simple dyspepsia. In fact, I felt terrible. At first I was concerned that I was not getting the rest I was going to need for the next day's hard work. And this was on a Monday night, so I was going to have to be on my toes for the rest of the week's demanding schedule. I needed my rest. But I wasn't getting it.

I was hot and threw off the bed covers. And yet I was also cold...my skin felt clammy. Something didn't seem right. In fact, not at all right. Well, er, my heart...it didn't seem to be beating right. There wasn't any real pain, nothing to knock me to my knees like a heart attack certainly... But something was wrong. And the more I considered it, the more severe the problem seemed to be. Still no real pain...but the very definite feeling that my body wasn't functioning right. I wondered about calling up Bud, Izzy, or Danny. I hesitated to bother them however because they needed their rest too and even more importantly, I didn't want to seem like a sissy-boy hypochondriac. What an idiot I would seem to be if I called one of them, got everyone all excited, took a trip to the hospital, and then was told that next time maybe I should order the medium or even small filet rather than the Mankiller Chunk o' Beef. No, I'd be better in the morning. I always had. For 55 years I had had just about every consequence of excess you can imagine but this good ol' bod of mine had always come through sooner or later.

The next morning I was down in the parking lot with my luggage at 7 just as we had all agreed, and I was ready to go. Sort of. I still felt pretty queasy but I don't think even at that point I said anything to anyone. We did the day's shoot and that evening

I took a pass on supper and just got some extra rest. If this was simply a matter of overeating or maybe a bit of blue cheese dressing that may have gone over the line, it sure didn't seem to be going away very fast. We did our television work the next day too, another complete story, and I got through it, although not with a lot of energy or enthusiasm. The story we shot on Wednesday, the next day, was about an artist working in brick, and we spent a good part of the day doing my on-cameras in the blazing heat of an airless brickyard where every stack of brick soaked up the sun's heat and threw it back at us.

At that point I told my friends on the crew that I was feeling pretty bad…maybe a touch of the flu, or just overwork, or…I don't know…maybe something I ate…. The next day I got through reading the sound track and the crew left me exhausted at home. I tried to rest that evening…it was now Thursday…but by now I was having some serious thoughts about what was going on inside me. Not only was something wrong, something very big was wrong. And I was pretty sure it was my heart.

Friday morning I told Linda something was definitely amiss with my innards and I thought we should go to the doctor right away. What I didn't tell her was what I feared it was, but it didn't matter: she had never before in our marriage of 20 years ever seen me volunteer to go to the doctor, even with broken bones. My old friend Doc Stanton gave us an immediate slot and took a quick listen to my heart. The look on his face told me what I already expected. He said we should go immediately to the hospital's emergency room, that he would call ahead and clear the way for us. There the doctors gave me a quick exam and confirmed that there was major trouble…my heart was firing on just two or three of its four cylinders and I was in real trouble. Atrial fibrillation it's called…heart chamber flutter. Instead of beating, a good part of my heart was just trembling and shuddering like an engine with a clogged sparkplug or broken intake valve stem. I would have to be admitted to the hospital at once for emergency treatment. There were looks of horror when I was asked when the problem had started and I had to admit my cosmic stupidity by saying, "Uuuuuh…five days ago…"

The doctors told Linda she might want to go home and pack up a suitcase of essentials for me for at least a week's stay in the hospital and then I had to admit my incredible lack of good sense to her by telling her, actually, she didn't need to go home to pack a bag for me. I had packed a bag and it was already in the trunk of the car. That is, I was admitting to her that I knew before we left the house that morning that I had serious cardiac problems and was headed for a hospital stay. I just hadn't bothered to tell her that reality. She was not comforted by my thoughtful preparations, I can tell you for a fact!

That led to a week in the hospital, some major philosophical considerations, and a few changes in life style. Of course the events of that week were serious. Potentially fatal afflictions usually are serious, at least to the person experiencing them. And yet there was inevitably a sense of the absurd, almost immediately from the beginning. After five days in a hospital bed, I was at the edge of apoplexy. I don't like medical stuff, I don't like hospitals, I don't like confinement, I loathe IVs, I hate bed pans, I do not want to be in bed all day unless it's at the demand of a long line of super models awaiting erotic satisfaction. Luckily, so far in my life I haven't had to face that particular dilemma, I'll have to admit.

I endured all I could. Once my heart was back on the job and my blood pressure had destabilized, all I could think of was getting out of that place. I know there are people who enjoy the attention of hospital care, find comfort in knowing that medical care is only a buzzer away, and even crave the kind of compassion that comes from illness… not me. I wanted the hell out of there now, and that was about all I could think of. It wasn't any one thing but about Wednesday or Thursday I decided that I had had about all the medical treatment I needed, or more precisely all the medical treatment, that I could stand.

Maybe the straw that broke this camel's back was the serious conversation I had with Linda about her future if it turned out I didn't have one. Even after everything had been dealt with in terms of my heart muscles, the long delay between the regular pulsing of my heart and my arrival at the hospital had given time for blood to pool in one of my heart chambers...and clot. If that clot should break loose and go to my brain...well, that would pretty much finish me off. The prognosis then was for a long period of care to dissolve the clot slowly, avoiding any premature breaking loose of it or its parts.

That's a problem. It's the kind of problem that kills you, in fact. I thought it was time to have a serious talk with Linda. I told her what was going on in my heart and expressed my sincere hope that if the worst did happen to me, that she would see our years together as a wonderful gift but move on with her own life. As I reminded her as our conversation continued, she is young, beautiful, and bright (and for that matter still is) and should seriously think of beginning life again...if possible with someone else worthy of her love. "I want you to understand," I told her, "that you should feel free to remarry. You owe me nothing, my lovely wife. When I am gone, if the chance comes along, feel perfectly free to marry another man..."

"Oh, Rog," she sobbed, "if the worst happens to you, there is no way I am going to marry someone else!"

"No, Linda, that's not the way I want it. We have enough assets to keep you solvent for as long as you need, but you shouldn't turn your back on life. Really...I want you to know you have my permission...which you really don't need, however...to remarry..." I said from my hospital bed.

"I don't even want to talk about this," she said, tears streaming down her face. "If you are gone, I have no intention of remarrying..."

"Linda, listen to me... It would not be fair to you or the world for you to shut yourself away. Just know now that my wish is for you not to rule out marriage when I am gone..."

"Oh no, Rog," she said, "I'm going to fool around... But I'm not about to get <u>married</u> again!"

Right then and there I resolved that I would, by God, get well again and stop that kind of talk right here and now. Man...does that woman have a bedside manner or what?! I should note here that Linda is a central character in my medical record as in my life and I recently told her so. She said "If that's the case, I want my name on the cover." I said that if I were to do that, she would make a lot more female friends since they would now sympathize with what her life with a grumpy old geezer had been like, but that no man reading the book would ever have anything to do with her. She said, "My plan is working."

At any rate, whatever the reason, I reached a point where I could no longer bear the invalid life in my hospital room and I told Linda I was getting dressed and getting out of there pronto, even if it meant "going over the wall."

Linda knows me well enough that she didn't argue. There is no arguing with me. I got dressed to the extent I could, we called the nurse in and told her I was leaving, she protested as best she could, I told her either she could take out the IV or I would but that whatever the case, I was leaving unless she thought she was big enough to stop me. I think she called a doctor who told her to go along with me, that apparently my heart was now strong enough to be thoroughly disagreeable...that is to say, I was getting back to normal.

However, at the hospital's main exit, I was stopped and prevented from leaving the building by a much burlier nurse with bulging biceps, an imposing mustache, and an authoritarian voice. She announced that I would not be leaving until I had paid my bill. Ah yes, the real Hypocritical Oath of the American medical system (at this writing the 37th best in the world, not the first unless you are stinking rich or in Congress, where you can enjoy the socialized medicine system that our criminal class reserves unto itself)—profit!

I took a seat at the dismissal desk. The woman there said I would not be able to leave today because it would take many hours to tabulate the precise balance of what I owed the hospital for the six days I had spent enjoying their hospitality. I said no, I was about to leave…within a quarter hour at the most and that they could either send me the bill when they finished their calculations… they knew after all where I lived and I had no intentions to abandon my farm just to avoid their billings.

Or I could tell her right then and there what the charges were.

She looked at me with complete disbelief…and maybe just a hint of contempt. "There is no way you can know what you owe," she said. "We have a complicated billing procedure. There are charges you can't possibly even know about. There are surcharges, taxes, procedural charges, tests, toothpicks, tissues, a bar of soap…"

"I owe you precisely $4,997.58," I said. "Write it down. I'll write you a check right here and now."

"You cannot possibly know what you owe. It will take me hours just to sort through everything, list it, and add it all up."

"No," I said. "Take it from me, I owe you $4,997.58. I'll write the check." And I started to write a check.

"Hold on. I'll tell you what I am going to do, Mr. Welsch," she said, almost sneering. "Just because you are so sure of yourself and because I know for a fact that there is no way whatsoever for you to precalculate such a figure, I'm going to drop everything right here and now and do a quick accounting right here and now on your charges... just to show you how wrong you are. Give me fifteen minutes," and she immediately set about doing a ferocious finger tap dance on her calculator. Papers flew, her computer began to overheat and glowed red with super-heat. Sweat beaded on her brow…and in almost exactly fifteen minutes she looked at me in complete astonishment…and now with just a hint of awe. "Your figure is," she said completely bewildered, "within three dollars of the actual total of your final bill. You owe us exactly $4995.27. How did you do that? That is simply not possible…"

"Easy," I smiled. "Our health insurance has a five thousand dollar deductible." And that, ladies and gentlemen, is a true story, so help me. Insurance companies know what they are doing and they are in the business of stealing from sick people. We pay premiums and they pocket the money. Then they use some of it to buy ads saying how kind and generous they are while at the same time hiring people to make damn sure they are not kind and generous. They buy huge computer systems with one single purpose…figuring out how not to pay your health bills. They are nothing more or less than casino owners, doing everything they can to pay out less money to the suckers than they are taking in, lying to you, screwing you, watching you suffer and die while they vacation at their homes in the Bahamas. Think of that the next time you vote for a politician who works to protect insurance company profits, you big dummies! I have written a lot of books over the years and I have learned the painful lesson that inevitably some things go out of date after a book is published, sometimes even before. I mention a woman who is at the moment considered a paragon of beauty and ten years…five years…one year later her name is an utter mystery to readers. Well, I hereby hope that by the time you read this, the above grumping is a total mystery to you: "What's he talking about? A national health care system? We have a wonderful full-care, single payer, universal health care system. Is this Welsch nut suggesting there was ever a time when we didn't? What the heck would people do if they didn't have a national single-payer health care system? Just get sick and die? Let other people get sick and die? What kind of barbarity would <u>that</u> be? No one would put up with that for long!"

Now, I want to make something clear here: while I am not at all crazy about spending time in a hospital, when the time comes that I need one, I'm sure happy it's there. I cringe however when I get a letter…as I did today…from a friend telling me that he has a problem and plans to go, as this guy tells me, to one of the top ten hospitals in the nation, where they have some of the top ten doctors in the world, where they serve their water only in crystal and their jello salads are prepared in a gourmet kitchens only by <u>cordon</u> <u>bleu</u> cooks. I mean, jeez, come on. Maybe if you have something really fancy wrong with you, you should go to a really fancy doctor in a really fancy hospital. But let's face it…a heart attack is a heart attack, a prostate is a prostate, a bellybutton hernia is a belly button hernia. Not only can just about any hack doctor in the country deal with these things, your local large animal veterinarian could probably take care of it just fine.

My buddy Woodrow just recent cut open his stomach. A huge gash, right across his gut when a huge, heavy glass table top he was shoving into his van broke and the razor-edge slashed open his belly from side to side. Our mutual friend Lunchbox rushed him to the nearest emergency ward where they sat waiting. He got tired of sitting around the big city emergency ward waiting room waiting for the doctors to finish lunch and a game of pitch—he walked down the hall finally, holding his intestines in place, until he found the doctors' lounge and went in to find out what the hell the hold up was…and that's what he found: lunch and pitch. So Woodrow had Lunchbox drive him on over to his place and patch him up. Lunchbox is an autobody repairman, which if you think about it a little bit isn't a long ways from a surgeon. So he used some strong adhesives he had in the shop to glue Woodrow's belly back together and then blew on the wound to dry out the mastic, serving a kind of double purpose too since as usual Lunchbox had been drinking pretty heavy that afternoon, which is probably why Woodrow cut open his belly in the first place, his breath not only warmed and dried the belly glue but sterilized it at the same time. Weeks later Woodrow went to a legit doctor to have the repair job checked and the doctor with the diplomas on the wall admitted he couldn't have done a better job.

Believe me, while I think it's grand that some people go to school to be doctors, I also think it's great that people go to school to learn how to repair auto engines. And frankly I don't think there's a dime's worth of difference between the two in the case of the vast…vast!…majority of afflictions you are likely to take into an emergency ward. I know people who have gone to the Mayo Clinic to get help for problems that could have been handled by an EMT in Dannebrog, except better, because the EMT didn't have a thousand other patients lined up in the hall waiting. And the patient near to home would have been more comfortable, better rested, and less exposed to all the other diseases and problems that come with traveling a long distance for medical care.

It's like hauling your old Allis Chalmer WC tractor from central Nebraska to a Lamborghini mechanic in Virginia to gap the spark plugs. It's overkill...and sometimes that isn't a metaphor. The Lambo mechanic is going to use the same size sockets to take off the valve cover, and the same thickness leaf gauge to check the gap, and the same screwdriver to tighten down the rocker arm adjustment. Except he won't take the time to do it right like the common old tractor mechanic up in town. And he'll charge you a thousand times more. And the results will be exactly the same.

You just can't tell me that the radiation accelerator used in my treatments in the little town just down the road on me last year (which I found out last week did the job, by the way) is somehow inferior to what have been used in Chicago. Yeah, if my prostate were really something special or my cancer somehow utterly unique to me, a fancy big city specialist might have been more appropriate. But I don't fool myself about such things. I'm an Allis Chalmers tractor, not a Lamborghini. A regular mechanic is just fine for my problems, and has pretty much the same tools as the fancy guys.

In fact, that isn't altogether accurate either, I guess. The doctors around here not only know their stuff just fine, and have the right tools to do the job, they also take the time to do the job right. I have always found the medical staffs around here willing to take whatever time it takes, or whatever time I want. They all know me by my first name, and where I live, and who Linda and Antonia are. Some of them even think of me as a friend.

Sometimes analogies like this are so close, they get to be creepy. The pretty blond nurse at the clinic...? Cheryl? Yeah, I know her. And she knows me. And man, do I ever trust her. Wanna know why? Because she restores old Allis tractors too. When she isn't assisting a doctor in probing around in some geezers innards, she's banging on old iron in her shop, twisting off rusted bolts, and welding up battered sheet metal. I may occasionally wonder if she is keeping my bum body parts well differentiated from the defective manifold she worked on just yesterday, but I've seen her work on her tractors and that gives me nothing but confidence about her work in the medical clinic.

Note too that I refer to her as "Cheryl." (And note too that all these names are fictitious and their descriptions and characterizations are invented from whole cloth.) As is the case with most of the medical people involved in my life, I know them by their first names. My GP is Ron. My oncologist is Bob. Our optometrist is Sue. I see them not only in their offices but now and then around town at a gas station or K-Mart or perhaps a fair or tractor show. I have enormous respect for their training and skill but what is even more important, I am not in awe of them. Nor do they expect such nonsense. They are pretty plain folks, just like me, and we are friends and acquaintances as well as me visiting them for their professional treatment and they reading my books and articles.

During one of my "cardiac incidents" I was away from home and wound up in the care of a doctor in a huge hospital…not my idea of where I want to be in any event…in a hospital…but definitely not a big hospital in a big city. So I was one of probably a couple hundred other people with the same problem on the same floor of this same hospital and I was pretty nervous about it. At least until I got to talking with the cardiologist and she asked where I am from. I told her I lived near the little village of Centralia, and she smiled that she knows the area well because she used to live just down the road fifteen minutes. She was reluctant to say much more but finally I squeezed it out of her. She was worried I might doubt her credentials because before she had gone into cardiology at med school, she had started as…a livestock manager trained on our State University's ag campus! Man, there's nothing that would give me more confidence than knowing that the doctor dealing with me knows her way around old bulls! That night I rested easy and slept well. Just as I've always wished, I was finally in the care of a certified animal doctor who studied at a cow college!

There can be, to be sure, some discomfort in having your doctors and nurses knowing you personally. There's such a thing as knowing too much about a patient. But one of the problems with being in a hospital is that it's not where you're accustomed to being...strange bed, strange food, strange light, strange sounds, strange people... But wait a minute! There is something you can do about that last item. You don't have to be surrounded by strange people. And we saw a report on television just last night that the average emergency ward wait in the United States today is four hours. Not in the country. You walk in, past the registration counter, and into the emergency room. My mother died a few days ago and we needed a death certificate signed. The man helping us simply drove down the street, spotted the doctor on a jog, rolled down his window, asked when she might be able to sign it, she said, "How about now?" and she signed it while keeping her cardio up by jogging in place. No one can convince me that the bigger the city, the bigger the hospital, the more assembly line the clinic, the better the medical care. It doesn't work that way at all.

Within many ethnic communities...in my experience on Native Reservations...sick people, especially dying people are cared for at home...on their bed, with the kind of food they are used to, surrounded by friends and family. In fact, there may be an intensification of these very factors...a holy man who is a neighbor and friend may come in to offer comfort...all day and night if needed. A group may gather outside the house or in another room to sing prayerful songs through the night. If the patient should wake up, he isn't confused by unfamiliar things. All around him are the things and people he knows and loves. Moreover, there won't be a feeling of despair and abandonment because he can hear the songs and prayers of his people right outside his door, and that tells him that everything that can and needs to be done is taken care of. And he rests easy.

If you are my age or older, you may remember a thing called "house calls." Doctors actually used to come to the patients' homes. That kept the patients comfortable and saved gigantic amounts of money by cutting down on the building of hospital rooms. Doctors still do house calls in most civilized countries. Not in the USA. We don't take none of that socialized medical care that catapults other countries ahead of us in health care, leaving us in the dust at 37th in the world…but first in money thrown into insurance industry pockets. And that's why we are tops in the world. Yep, the good ol' US&A is number one for stupidity.

All my life I have been a storyteller and as we drove home from the hospital, despite my anxiety and discomfort, even in the face of the sudden wake-up call that after all my convictions to the contrary I am mortal, I anticipated that whatever else all this cardiac misery had caused me, I am going to have one heck of a story to tell everyone back at the Chew 'n' Chat Café. But as you will find when you come back to your customary environment with your own tales of medical adventures, the first liar is always at a disadvantage.

I should have known that. I've spent half my life out here in the rural countryside and one of the first things I learned and the one thing I have learned for absolute certain, you don't go waltzing into any gathering the morning after a good rain and announce something hopelessly stupid like "I got a half inch over at my place last night; how much rain did you get at your place?" I quickly learned that no matter how much I got in my rain gauge, almost everyone else at the table had more. The protocol, it turns out, is to answer the question "How much did you get?" with "How much did you get?" or "Not as much as I'd hoped…what did you get?" I either had to learn how to lie better or to put up two rain gauges just to keep up with the competition.

It turns out that the same competition rules pertain with geriatric health problems: whatever you have, someone else has had it worse. You have a double hernia, Ray has a triple hernia. You had a triple bypass, Verne had a octagonal polyhedral bypass. Your blood pressure topped out at 228/177, Ralph's was a safety-valve popping 443/289. You got a stent; Larry had open heart surgery –the procedure being conducted through his left ear. Your PSA is 18.4, Tom's is 27.6. It's amazing. The doctor told you that your condition was critical and that you needed immediate medical attention...well, every single one of your buddies has had it worse, felt no particular discomfort, went through much more drastic procedures, and managed to recuperate without whining about it, not one complaint from one single person... and certainly no hopeless complaining like you are doing. So, my first advice once you have had your examination, gone through your test results, and have set up a protocol of treatment for any major health problem in your Geezer years is not to give out any details. At least not right up front. Strike up a conversation at the tavern, after church, over coffee at the café, sometime during a reunion or family gathering and casually mention that you have always wondered if any of the men present haves any experience with, say, with atrial fibrillation.

Listen patiently to everyone else's narratives. Hear everyone out. Don't let temptation lead you to jumping in with your own stories. Nod. Look sympathetic. It wouldn't even hurt to jot down some of the figures mentioned just to be sure you won't be outbid later when you start dropping some details of your own.

Then... there!... open up about your medical problems, but don't be too quick even at that point with your details. Hold your trump cards until you can be fairly confident that everyone else has spilled his or her own medical holdings before you throw your cards on the table and yell "Gin!" and pronounce that...your health problems are worse than theirs. Not just a little worse. A lot worse. Your symptoms are much more dramatic. Your treatments are infinitely more extreme and humiliating. In fact, what you have been going through is so much worse than what these other sissies are complaining about, you don't even feel comfortable telling the whole story. This strategy won't make you any friends but it'll sure help you maintain your self respect and maybe even get you some sympathy from bystanders who are young and/or healthy enough not to understand the game.

And that's important because if your friends and family are anything like mine, the only sympathy you're likely to get is going to be from outsiders. I was still in the hospital just days after my cardiac "incident" or "event" happened (See? Even the medical system is in on this effort to diminish whatever sympathy you have coming, the only compensation there is for physical problems after all, by giving them names like "incident" instead of the far more dramatic "impending doom and disaster")... Where was I? Oh yeah...I was still in the hospital when the word leaked out and got back to the streets of the little town where I live. The first visitors I had to my hospital room cheerfully reported to me that there were already efforts in my circle of friends to do a security inventory of the tools in my shop for me, to check on the condition of the bottles in my wine cellar, and to stop by for regular checks on my widow...uh, wife. The single most common comment about my heart problems was not a word of sympathy but an expression of surprise that I even had a heart.

As if it weren't enough that Linda asked me at one point if I thought it would be socially permissible to include a sale bill for the auction in with my funeral notice to save printing costs, I was told confidentially by a friend that he had happened to be in the local newspaper office the very day when Linda was also there. He reported to me that she asked the clerk at the newspaper how much an obituary would cost...if the worst should come to pass and I died from my heart problems. The clerk said, "The cost of an obituary is a dollar a word...but the first five words are free." My friend said that he was pretty sure he heard Linda then say, "Okay...make it 'Rog died...tractors for sale.'"

We never know when our time might come. Sometimes by another person's hands. I have always noted that never in the history of all mankind has a woman shot a husband who was at the time washing dishes. Just a simple hint for survival to my fellow man. A woman near here was once reported to have tried to hire a gunman to kill her husband and as such things seem to always go, the gunsel she found was…an undercover cop. I asked Linda on that occasion if she would ever hire someone to shoot me. I was only slightly comforted when she answered, "Gosh, no, Rog. I'd just go up town and ask for volunteers."

I strongly advocate making, as they gently put it, "prior arrangements." It definitely takes a lot of strain off your loved ones because otherwise they have to make hard decisions for you, and that's just not a manly way to do it. In fact, I have begun to give various of my treasures…mostly interesting sticks and rocks…to people I want to have them. Which is probably one of the reasons I was once advised not to have a military funeral because it might prove difficult in this little town to find four guys for an honor guard who wouldn't shoot into the coffin. Also, in checking about cremation as a final disposal of my remains I was warned that it really might not work because it would take so long to put out the grease fire.

We have had mountain lions cruising through our river bottoms now and again and for many years I thought it would be great to die down there; I told Linda that if I didn't come back from a walk some time she should just wait a week or so while the lions did their work. Then I thought she could gather up some lion scat (poop, in the venacular) in a paper bag and at the memorial service just have the sack of cat scat (say it ten times as fast as you can) on the altar as my remains. A friend said that just would not suit my personality or habit. He suggested that they gather the scat in the bag, put it on someone's front porch, light it on fire, ring the door bell and run for cover. He was probably right.

The problem for anyone suffering a medical affliction in America, especially if the patient is male and elderly, is that somehow that combination automatically turns everyone into a stand-up comedian. You are genuinely concerned about what will happen to your sex life now that you have experienced a serious heart problem. You ask the doctor a serious question. What does he say? He says, "It's okay to have sex as long as you don't get too excited. It would probably be best therefore to pretty much stick with your wife." And he laughs uproariously, not at all troubled by the facts that 1) you have a real physical problem and 2) that's just about the oldest joke in the world.

Another doctor from another town but who knew about me and heard about my cardiac problems wrote and suggested, helpfully, that I could sure cut down on medical costs by skipping any consideration of resorting to a defibrillator, that zapper you see them using on television medical shows where the attendants plant the paddles on the unconscious patient's chest, shout "Clear!" and then send a jolt of electricity to the heart to jar it back into regularity. This doctor told me that I could get the very same effect by starting up one of my old Allis Chalmers WC tractors, slowing it down to as low an idle as I could get, wetting my fingers and grabbing a sparkplug wire. I told him that I appreciated his "help."

So, shouldn't at least your wife take a serious view of the situation? I mean, okay, sure, she's a candidate to inherit one hell of a lot of insurance money, not to mention the remote channel changer for the television set, an exercise of power she has lusted for now for decades, but who's going to open jars and kill spiders for her when you're gone? Oh yeah...there are all those buddies of yours who have already volunteered to make regular stops after the funeral to check on her, uh, welfare.

Again, I should have known. Long before I sensed Geezerhood coming upon me Linda and I were in a conversation up at the tavern with several other couples about our same age. For some reason we got to talking about what each of us would do if our mate died and the conversation was fairly serious, even philosophical, until one guy...a real jerk...sneered that by God, if he should die and his wife ever had anything to do with some other man, he would come back from the dead, haunt her bedroom, and make her sex life miserable. Her response probably anticipated the divorce that came along later that same year: "The more things change, the more they stay the same."

As I noted before, up to this time in my life I had dropped by my doctor's office once a year or so, not really paying much attention to my regularity in such visits, sometimes missing a year or two here and there. But once you go through the door into Geezerhood, visits to your doctor(s) become the very substance of your social life. You know receptionists and nurses by their first names and they recognize you even when seeing nothing more than the open back of your hospital gown as you trudge down the hall from one monitoring machine to the next. They might just as well leave a tap in your arm for drawing the regular blood samples needed for common blood medicines like Coumadin…which is after all nothing more than the most common form of rat and mouse poison you can buy off the shelf. When I was finally told I could stop taking the stuff and go instead to a regular, light dosage of aspirin, I asked my doctor what I should do with all the left-over Coumadin pills I had in my bathroom medicine cabinet. "Toss 'em under your chicken house," he said. "They're good for clearing out the mice." Coumadin is a blood thinner and so requires constant monitoring… which means sampling your blood. Now, I don't mind bleeding. I'd be surprised if I didn't cut myself just sitting here writing this morning, and I'll flick the blood off on the floor and continue with what I'm doing. But a few drops pulled from my arm with a needle…I go green and go down. It's called "measuring your pro-time," and you can take it from me that many of the blood-letters are anything but pros. You will come to dread the words "whoops," "ouch, " and "sorry." The experts go in with the slightest tick of pain and are backing out in moments with a 5-gallon bucket of blood at their feet. Others go looking for a vein as if they were fishing out the last bit of peanut butter at the bottom of a jar. Look, at this writing I am 73 years old. I am now asking that everything I have to go in for this torture, they just lop off one bit of a finger at the knuckle and drain what they need into an open bucket. I am old enough and have enough knuckles that this arrangement should work until blood tests are no longer needed.

But I'm not the kind who simply becomes a victim and suffers silently. I developed a few useful strategies of my own as my cardiac treatment moved along. For example, I was instructed not to have more than one drink a day from that point on. With the help of my buddies however we figured out that when I was working around the house or in my office, that limitation could be easily met simply by mixing up a five- or six-gallon bucket of gin and tonic around noon and nursing it along until bed time. When carrying around my bucket wasn't convenient and I perhaps found myself at the town tavern with my pals, we devised a system by which I would order a beer…one only!…and then exercise extreme caution not to finish it but have the barkeep "freshen it up" every ten minutes or so. Technically therefore it was always still the same drink and I could in all honesty report to my doctors… and not so incidentally to Linda… that I was being a good boy and was indeed faithfully observing my one-drink-a-day limit.

I was not so successful in meeting my cardiologist's stern instruction that I would have to eliminate the stress in my life as soon as possible. As I told him, "Look, doc, I've been married to her for twenty years now and it's going to take me a little time to figure out how to cut the ties and get her to fill the freezer with casseroles so I won't starve to death the first month she's gone." Linda was in the office with me at the time and I thought for sure she'd be flattered and even charmed by my demonstration of consideration for her feelings. She wasn't.

Now, if you are of the feminine persuasion and are about to get indignant about my sexist attitudes, save your breath because Lovely Linda, if anything, out guns me when it comes to the wise remarks category. This very morning Linda was commenting on her usual morning blahs ("Hey Rog, do you ever wake up grumpy?" "Nah, I usually get up quietly and try to sneak out before she realizes I'm gone") and said, "Mornings, I like to sit here drinking coffee until the pain is gone…never for a moment forgetting that it won't be long before he's back with the mail."

As I hope I have made clear by now, Linda is not exactly defenseless in this battle of the sexes. Just a couple weeks ago the television news was filled with a struggle of a young woman to welcome the dignity of death in the face of the rantings of manipulative politicians and the agony of hysterical parents. At some point I turned to Linda and said, "Hon, I hope that you will have the strength and good sense to pull the plug on me when the time comes for me to move along..." and without hesitation she reached around and groped behind my chair as if trying to find a switch.

I wasn't done with this particular chapter of my life—affairs of the heart. A few years later, also while working too hard, under stress, on the road, not paying much attention, I had yet another cardiac "event"—same thing—atrial flutter. And once again I took that ride to the hospital emergency room. This time the piece de resistance was a camera jammed down my throat to take a look at my heart without interference from things like ribs. I suppose that's better than going in to take a look by way of any other orifice, or perhaps making a new opening, but it sure wasn't any fun having a gigantic hose stuffed down my throat.

At least that's what they tell me. I can't say because I don't remember. Curiously, that's how such things are sometimes handled these days. See, they can anesthetize you so you don't feel the pain or know what's happening, but for this process, for reasons I don't recall, the doctors and technicians need you to be awake and aware, so what they do is put you through the hell of this procedure but then dose you with the same stuff they call the "date-rape drug" so that while you do experience all the misery and discomfort as the horrendous operation is being done, *you don't remember it when it's over!*

I think that is an absolutely stunning notion about pain, and instructive regarding geezerhood in general. Pain is not simply what you experience, it's *what you remember about the pain after it's over!* Isn't that amazing? So all you really need to do about all the woes and trials of getting older, is to do whatever you can to forget them! And then it's as good as if they didn't happen at all! Excuse all the exclamation marks but I find each and every sentence of this paragraph to be astonishing. But, well, uh...now I can't remember why.

Moreover, during this round of medical treatment I found new hope in where our otherwise miserable American medical system is headed. Despite the baloney politicians tell you about our medical delivery system being the best in the world, it is actually 37th, damn near down among the pathetic non-systems of the Third World...unless you are stinking rich or politicians enjoying the benefits of the "socialized medicine" they deny *you,* and that you, by the way, are paying for. A standard comment of mine for years has been that I would prefer to get my medical attention from our local rural veterinarian if only he had a squeeze chute big enough for me.

Once I was again stabilized I was sent home with instructions to set up preparations with my usual cardiologist in the hospital near our home for a procedure called a "catheterization," a process that sends a tube up into your heart to measure various functions, rotorooter out clogs, or expand blood passages. (In my case they were just looking around, seeing how things were going, finding out exactly what the problem might be in there so I was spared the part where they put an balloon on the end of the tube and then blow it up to expand arteries. Nope, they were saving the balloon-on-the-hose trick for a later humiliation in my medical adventures.)

Again, the catheterization process was no fun but by now I had learned my lesson that medical procedures in Geezerdom always work under the theory that the cure should be worse than the problem. I was getting used to having mechanical devices stuck into my poor old body somewhere or another...rear end, mouth, ears, nose, veins...so I was prepared for almost anything. But I'll have to admit that I was a bit surprised when I showed up to have this glorified sewer snake sent into my heart to find that everything I had been told before by traditional wisdom, that "the way to a man's heart is through his stomach" is not at all true. As it turns out...and this will not come as a surprise I suppose to a lot of people...the way to a man's heart is through his groin.

I had already experienced the obvious exception when doctors took a look at my heart with the down-the-hatch camera, and now the nurses prepping me for this operation were shaving…what?!…my inner <u>thigh</u>?! What the hell is <u>that</u> all about? Is this maybe a misunderstanding? "Excuse me, Nurse," I said, "but I'm here for a catheterization, not a hernia repair or vasectomy. Shouldn't you be shaving my chest? Or is this just some recreational work?"

"Spread your legs," she said seductively. "And hold your breath for ten minutes."

I hadn't had a lot of my geezerly medical experiences at this point but I'd had enough that I was already wondering about the kind of sense of humor typical to the nursing profession. Isn't it just a little suspicious that nurses are always doing things that require you to wear those idiotic hospital gowns, for example? And why exactly do they insist on taking your temperature by sticking the thermometer…well, you know? Why is it always a woman who "preps" you for an operation, a medical euphemism for shaving your embarrassing parts? And why do they use lather and razors? I suppose I should be grateful they do de-fur the area with a razor and lather rather than bikini wax or eyebrow tweezers. (Ow!) A secret to my enormous success in almost every area into which I have ventured is to skip the unimportant people in any system and go directly to those who actually run things. That is, not the "suits," executives, CEOs, chairpersons, bosses, owners, managers, etc., but the secretaries and nurses. Think about it, if you are going to kiss butts to get things done, whose strikes you as being the nicest to consider kissing…some fat guy in a suit or some lovely in a nurse's uniform?

My theory is that nursing is a tough occupation as it is. These nice ladies are constantly dealing with people who are sick and unhappy. Moreover, human bodies are pretty much the same, coming only in two basic models—male and female. Sure, there are young and old bodies, fat and skinny, brown and pink, blah blah blah, but other than that, it's not at all like a veterinarian who deals one day with goats, cows, and dogs and the next with parrots, cats, and horses. Now, <u>that</u> is variety. No, a nurse in a medical doctor's office not only winds up looking at the same two models of human manufacture day after day but probably has some sort of specialty and therefore winds up looking at the same <u>part</u> of the anatomy day after day, and maybe even primarily only the same part of the same model every day. At least an auto mechanic gets the variety of different years, different models, different makes. Not a nurse. It's the same thing every day…feet, feet, feet…boobs, boobs, boobs…noses, noses, noses…left butt cheek, left butt cheek, left butt cheek.

Isn't it understandable therefore that those who inhabit the world of nursing do what they can to insert the slightest bit an interesting variety into their lives? It sure makes sense to me. So here comes a guy…let's call him ol' Rog…who needs a shot. You can give it to him anywhere on his body, which gives you about ten acres to choose a spot the size of a needle point. How about his arm? Or maybe his finger? Well, he's a kind of annoying guy anyway, and there are people out there in the waiting room who can see through the open door, so why not humiliate this big bozo <u>and stick the needle in his butt</u>?!

I think that's the way the nurse-thinking went when it came to determining the entry point for the tube for my catheterization. Here's Rog, and we are going to send a tube into his heart. We are going to go into his heart from somewhere outside this body, making pretty much our own entrance, which means that we can pretty much put the in-door wherever we want to. So let's just scout around through the brush and terrain and pick a spot that is not only convenient for us but as embarrassing as possible for the guy with the big mouth.

Having only had one of these procedures myself I can't say for sure, but my suspicion is that the nurses get together before an operation like this and talk it over. In my imaginings, the conversation goes something like this:

"Look, we're going to have to shave a couple square feet..or maybe yards… of this guy, so let's make it easy on ourselves, okay? No fanny work this time."

"We've done plenty of neck artery entries lately, so that sure isn't any fun. How about his arm pit?"

"Man, I don't know…that's some pretty gnarly braid there. Do we have a razor tough enough to deal with rope like that?"

"Yeah, and there's always the danger with a farm boy like Rog that he spent the day before the operation cutting wood and has developed something of an armpit wang about him too. Maybe we should consider a more…uh…congenial area."

"Look, isn't this that Welsch guy who wrote that male sexist claptrap bragging about how much he knows about women…what was it?… something like <u>Everything I Know About Women</u>… How about let's really humiliate this one and shave his naughty bits for him."

"Yeah, that's a great idea. Let's see how macho he is when he knows that razor is only a fraction of an inch away from Mr. Happy…and is being scraped back and forth across his groin by a woman!"

"Hey, that's a great plan!"

"Terrific…his crotch it is! And how about all three of us do the honors and maybe giggle a little why we do the shaving so he can't tell exactly what it is we're laughing about! And my guess is that we'll have plenty to laugh at."

"Exactly! And why not shave a little happy face into his belly hair just for the fun of it!"

"Yea!"

"Hooray!"

"Wow, I thought tomorrow was going to be just another boring day at the clinic and now I'm actually looking forward to this procedure!" "And then…<u>let's charge him $50 for *three* disposable razors!</u>" [General hilarity, gleeful planning, high fives all around… Cue "The Fight Song" from the RoseAnn Barr School of Nursing…]

Now, don't get me wrong. I adore nurses. And even if you don't, the last thing you want to do when under medical care is to annoy the nurses unless you want to find yourself enjoying bed pans brought to you direct from the hospital deep freezer, IV needles the size of railroad spikes, and sponge baths with wire brushes. Nurses have seen…and done…everything. The last thing they need in their day is someone who thinks a hospital is a luxury spa and they are two-dollar an hour servants. My advice…keep it light and easy. Do what you can to help. Joke, but make yourself the butt of the joke, and it will pretty much come down to your butt in all likelihood anyway. Oh, I flirt but I don't get fresh. You will find that they have a code of humor too, with some pretty funny lines. I was about to have an invasive cardiac procedure performed and while I was being reassured, I noted that I was a lot more concerned about the insertion of the IV than the knife cut for the incision. I had already established an atmosphere of good humor with the nurses, as I usually do. A nurse came in, for example, to take my temperature with one of those sensors they stick in your ear. I remarked to the young woman, "You'd be amazed if I told you where they used to stick a thermometer to get a patient's temperature." Okay, funny guy… But then she said, "Know the difference between an oral and an anal thermometer?" I said no. She said simply, "The taste." Nurse joke.

So I should have been prepared but wasn't when the nurse came in to insert the intravenous needle into my arm, knowing my total aversion to the process. "Okay," she said, waving the needle around. "Try to be patient with me. This is my first time!" I turned green. She laughed. She was pimping me and got me but good. I laughed then and felt a lot better about submitting my queasiness to her well practiced and skillful hands.

Three years in a row I wound up in a cardiac hospital on or around Valentine's Day…I told everyone the PaceMaker was a special gift for Linda but believe me, roses and chocolates would be cheaper. Anyway, my last "procedure" fell on Mardi Gras, so I took along a sack of beads to strew around as they wheeled me down the hall to the operating room. I gave all the nurses strings of beads, which they cheerfully put around their necks. It was all very colorful. They rolled my gurney into an elevator and I handed out more beads to the three lovelies transporting me to the knife session and a pretty nurse named Dawna said, "Oh thank you! And I didn't even have to earn them!" "Earn them?"

the other two asked. "Sure," she explained, and tugged up the front of her blouse (but without actually bringing this sick old man real cheer by lifting it over her head...I think it was something about not wanting to kill me before the actual operation even started).

Once the other wonderfully innocent Nebraska girls realized how one customarily "earns" Mardi Gras bead strings, they started to pull them from their necks but I stopped them and said that it was giving me such a grand reputation around the hospital I wondered if they might not just leave them on for the day and let people in the halls, wards, and offices go ahead and guess. And they did.

My dream is to get enough money together sometime that I can check out of a hospital and make a general announcement, "This Saturday 8 p.m. drinks will be free at the Slobbery Raccoon Tavern for all you nurses who took care of me the past week." I can only imagine the great jokes and stories I would collect in those couple hours. I mean, wow, nurses must have great parties! And there might be other benefits. Who knows? As I was being finished up after having a PaceMaker installed, that gorgeous blond nurse named Dawna asked me where I was headed and I said back to my home on the beautiful Loup River, in a picturesque log cabin in the woods. Almost pleadingly she stopped, looked at me, and said, "Kidnap me." I was sooo tempted.

The time did come when several doctors and cardiologists had children getting to an age where they were ready for college, one felt the time had arrived for his dream trip on a single-malt tasting tour of Scotland, and one had a big payment due on a boat, so they decided I needed a PaceMaker, a little distributor buried in your chest that sends out electrical impulses to keep your heart pumping at a regular rate. There was also a rich irony no one should miss that a winter was quickly passing during which both our septic tanks had continued work and the well was still pumping. And what's a Nebraska winter without a family catastrophe of no particular anecdotal value? So it was decided I would go bionic and become….Robo Rog!

There were the usual consultations, Q&As, and detailed and unwelcome descriptions of what I was in for. I of course hoped that PaceMakers had come far enough to have added functions… after all, telephones do a lot more than provide communications these days…so I thought maybe I could get one installed that would also open garage doors or work as a television channel selector. Or male enhancement aid? Linda asked the doctors to turn up the gain on the attitude dial. We got little help along these lines.

It was amazing that once I let out the word about the PaceMaker that I got reports from everywhere. I had hoped I would have a unique affliction and be able to show off my mechanical device, as it were, to young ladies up at the town tavern, but the glow was lost once it turned out that these days people have PaceMakers like they have cell phones. Most device wearers spoke of how they had changed their lives positively but others were less encouraging. Old friend Verne reported when he told his mechanic friend Emil that his father was getting a Pacemaker, the old bolt-twister said with a serious mien, "Pacemakers don't work. Just take a metal detector to a cemetery sometime. They're all over the place."

I did what I could to rescue something positive from the PaceMaker procedure. When the lovely and sultry Svetlana showed up with her razor to shave…what else?…my crotch, I noticed that she was a bit uneasy about moving around the furniture, so to speak, with one hand while wielding her razor with the other. Trying to be helpful…I always am…I suggested that maybe it would easier if she held the equipment up out of the way while I did the shaving. She allowed as how she didn't think that fell within the accepted protocols for crotch shaving. Gotta hate red tape.

There have been surprising consequences to wearing a PaceMaker. Something no one mentioned before they sold us on the device is that once one is installed, the wearer can no longer arc weld. That's something of an inconvenience for a guy who has a shop and arc welds. Nor can I use a chainsaw. Again, a bit of a problem for someone who has a tree farm, heats a three large buildings with wood stoves, and has four chainsaws. I checked with all manner of experts about this, if some shielding might not be available, would electric saws be okay, a lead vest? How serious are those rules? One doctor, seriously, recommended that I could go ahead and use a chainsaw but to be sure to stop welding as soon as I passed out. Good thinking.

On the other hand, and to our amazement, the way they check to make sure the Pacemaker (Verne's mother calls his dad's his "Pacer"), is by telephone. No kidding. They call, you put on two expandable bracelets, lay the phone receiver on a box, and bingo, they know how it doing. Now…when are they going to figure out how to take pro-time blood tests over the phone?

About six months after the Pacemaker was installed I was instructed to return to the clinic so that the manufacturer's representative could do a major check-up of how their device was working. Which struck me as a great idea. Along the way I had become rather attached to the device that regulated my heart and that I was counting on to keep me alive. I was sat down in a quiet room and yet another pretty lady attached various electrodes to me, all the while chatting pleasantly. She plugged me into her computer and her little printer device began chugging out a strip of paper, which she looked at, humming comfortingly. It took a while and a lot of paper rolled through that printer. I supposed there must be a lot of readings to be taken. Then she started saying things that were, to say the least, curious: "Mr. Welsch, you are doing quite well but I can see that you had a bit of trouble the morning of March 16th. That seems to have stuck with you about six hours. And then again on May 3 and 5 you had some trouble…apparently overnight. Did you have some sort of problem during the first three days of June?"

"Well, uh, yes. That was when I was up in town for the village festival and worked a lot longer than I intended to and got a lot more tired than I should have and… But…wait… Are you telling me this device in here [taps shoulder] is recording everything I do?"

"Yes," she said sweetly. And then disconcertingly smiled, blinked, and said, "In fact, we wind up knowing a lot more about our patients than we probably should. Or really want to." Teeheehee....

You mean, like...you know...when Linda and I... Yes. That's right. Everything. Right there on the read-out tape. All affairs, as it were, of the heart, so to speak, are kept track of electronically in the Pacemaker and then are spit out on paper for some young lady to read and appreciate. Or not appreciate.

Being a writer with an active and fairly successful imagination, I began to think that maybe it would be a good idea for a lot of men...not me, of course!...to be cautious about inviting their wives along for such check-ups and Pacemaker read-outs. I imagined a scenario:

Pacemaker Tech Expert: "Well, I can see we had a little bit of major fun about noon on October 15th, didn't we?"

Standerby Wife: "No, that can't be right. Arnold was at that boring business convention with his secretary Heidi in Des Moines on October 15th, isn't that right, Arnold?"

Arnold: "I, uh, right...I was in a sales seminar and..."

Techie: "No, it is quite clear here on the read-out. It says that about 7 that evening you had a bit too much to drink...it's just a guess but I'd say those are champagne bubbles I see there...then there was a crescendoing period of arousal and excitement, and then... Yep. No doubt about it. I've read a thousand of these things and I know a seismic orgasm when I see one."

As busy as Linda is, I'm sure not going to use up her precious time by taking her to my next Pacemaker checkup. I don't want her to see how close I was to a coronary when that last goal was scored in the Stanley Cup playoffs. For those of you who keep a weekly appointment for, as Linda calls it, kicking down the accelerator, when the computer lady asks what the heck it is you do at 2 o'clock every Friday afternoon, tell her that's when your bowling league meets.

# THE BIG C:

Cancer Cancer Cancer Cancer Cancer…

There, I've said it, the ugliest word in the English language. Cancer Cancer Cancer Cancer. Now, that wasn't so hard, was it? I have no idea what it is about cancer that generates so much fear and awe but there's not much doubting that it does. Maybe it's because cancer has such low visibility…it's a kind of "stealth" affliction. Or maybe it's because it so often is the final punctuation mark on what one has always presumed is a run-on sentence. It's entirely possible that the dread that is so much a part of coming down with cancer is that everyone knows that the methodologies for attacking that accursed evil are damn near as bad as the problem itself. The moment you are diagnosed with cancer, you really don't care one way or another <u>why</u> it is so feared an attack on your body: all you know is that this wasn't your idea of the way you wanted the diagnosis to go.

In my case at least it was a long story winding up with a thoroughly unsatisfactory punch line, sort of like those endless narratives they used to call "shaggy dog stories." You know, the ones that go on and on and on and then wind up with a really stupid and decidedly unfunny punch line that makes it clear the person telling you the story really didn't want to amuse you as much as to make you feel that you had been duped into listening to something that really wasn't worth the time and effort. There's a reason jokes like that are called "groaners." In my case, cancer has been a sort of morbid groaner.

I had had one minor brush with the Ugly C when a biopsy on a lump on one ear went sour. But you know, hey…what's an ear?! It sticks out there…at least mine do…and losing one wouldn't be all that bad a deal, especially for us over-age hippie long-hairs. Just another comb-over. In fact, to my mind, that was going to be the problem. If you are going to have cancer, and it appears we all will at one time or another, it should be worth a major production of sympathy. I mean, jeez…IT'S *CANCER!*

So I started the rumor mill working around here about my afflicted ear as best I could, but even early on there was precious little compassion to be found. Men are like that. And, well, so are women, I guess. My buddies said that with ears like mine, a bit of a trim shouldn't be a problem; Linda spread the word that she was having my ear notched like ranchers do with cattle, just another identification feature to help her keep track of me.

So, they cut off the afflicted part of the ear and sewed it up. And at that moment the doctor said something that sent a cold chill down my spine: "There you go, Roger. I'm pretty good at this, so there shouldn't even be a scar." Oh no! I have cancer, I go through all this trouble, I pay all this money, I have all these anxieties…and…I wind up with no visible scar I can use to generate sympathy?! Talk about the injustice of life! Why me?! Why do I always have to be the one who looks fine?!

It was some years after that exercise in oncological futility that I went to see my GP for a regular, or maybe sort-of regular check-up, and as part of the look-see they took a blood sample. Fine. When the results came in a few days later the doctor went through the results with me and recommended that I go to a urologist and have another test or two because my PSA, a measurement of an enzyme present in the blood when prostate cancer is doing its ugly work, was somewhat elevated…nothing drastic but enough so that it would be a good idea to exercise some caution. Okay, still so far, so good.

We got an appointment then with a doctor I came to know and love as "Doctor Midget Digit." You would think that one of the first things you would take into account when considering a career involving checking on something well up gentlemen's rear ends...a curious career choice in any event, you'll have to admit...you would think that before...<u>before</u>...deciding not to check the boxes that could steer your training in the direction of seeing lovely young women naked but instead choosing the one that involves exploring fat guys' butts (I truly apologize for the crudity of this section but believe me, it's going to have to get worse because there is absolutely nothing dignified about where I am taking you in this chapter)...you would think that one of the first things you would take a look at when deciding on a career in buttology is the suitability of the one asset you will need most in your chosen line of work...the length of your forefinger. There is something to be said about the courage, determination, and extra effort of someone like a former soundman I had in a network television crew who was deaf as a post...I mean, you have to admit, being deaf while working with <u>sound</u> constitutes something of a challenge. But one must also recognize that when you are depending on the skill, training, and capability of someone you count on to judge the quality of sound, you have to hope he has some ability to hear the damn sounds you are making. That is to say, a <u>sound</u> technician should be able to hear no matter how insistent the idiots are who demand that we all be considered equal <u>even when it is clear that we are not.</u>

Same with a doctor who is about to stick his finger up your butt. While there is, to be sure, a certainly amount of amusement for those of us who enjoy irony, when the doctor after putting considerable effort into his assignment...a dedication to his work that you cannot see but clearly sense in the moment...speaks to you from behind and over your shoulder while you lean in humiliation over an examining table after he has spent what seems like hours trying to reach your tonsils through your rear end...says, "I'm not able to reach your prostate. I'll have to call in someone else," and leaves you leaning over his examination table, your pants down around your ankles, your bare fanny cooling under the air conditioning vent while his nurse tries to focus her attention on the whine of the country music playing over the clinic Muzak system, your sense of humor quickly weakens.

Call in someone else? What? Are there urology and proctology specialists who are kept around in case someone needs a finger long enough to reach the damn gland they are supposed to specialize in examining?! That's like taking your car to a mechanic who says, "You'll have to leave it here for a week until I can find someone with a wrench." Note to any pre-med student considering any line of work that involves digital examinations of rectal orifices (and it is my experience that every single male affliction requires exactly that approach to the problem, including excessive ear wax, male pattern balding, and toenail fungus—always—always!—they approach the problem through one's nether eye): Before you decide on a career in medicine, please...Take a good long, hard look at your blasted index finger. Is it a stubby little digit that would clearly disqualify you for playing the guitar? Then take it from someone who knows whereof he speaks, and stay the hell out of proctology, urology, buttology, assology, anusology, kiesterology, or any other line of work that requires backdoor work. I'm sure that somewhere there's a job meant for you and those stumps you call fingers... maybe installing thumbtacks on school bulletin boards or tamping kosher dills into jars over at the pickle factory, but please...please!...save yourself and a lot of other people like me the discomfort of trying to make yourself into something you have clearly been denied by God.

Anyway, Doctor Midget Digit called in Doctor Dinglefinger and they...well, they did what they had to do. It was behind my back so I can't really say for sure what it was. And they took more blood. And they looked that all over and said that I would need to come back to their office again because they both still had more kids to put through college, a hike in the country club dues, and the constant dunning for payments on the boat, and so they needed the money. Actually, that's not what they said but by this time I was getting to be very good at interpreting such situations. They said I now needed a colonoscopy, a procedure involving sending a very small camera into my innards…and once again, guess where the tollbooth to the turnpike leading to this adventure is located.

That's right…my exhaust vent, as it were. And here's where you really start to understand Einstein and his theory of relativity. Didn't the doctor just say "a very small camera?" Well, what he has come to think of as a very small camera <u>in his hand</u> is not at all what you are going to consider a "very small camera" when the doctor and his assistants Bruno and Ilsa shove it up your…well, let's just say shove it. You will think for all the world that for this special occasion they didn't just settle for a tiny camera…no… along with the camera they sent in and up a soundman, producer, gaffer, key grip, and best boy, if not also a caterer and wardrobe designer. I believe this is an excellent example of Einstein's theory of relativity: items stuffed up your rear end seem much larger to the shovee than to the shover.

I don't know if it would help or not if the doctor told you this, but I'm going to because I really think you should know—again in the spirit of relativity-- yes, a colonoscopy is incredibly uncomfortable. Even worse, it is embarrassing. Especially if somewhere there behind you someone laughs. Especially if it's the teenage cutie the doctor just introduced to you as "Heidi, a community college student who's thinking of going into buttular technology." You can take some comfort that after this experience of a Journey to the Center of Roger, student Heidi will almost certainly check the career-choice box for "dental assistant" or "manicure specialist" when finally deciding on a life career. But it is all relative. There is some good chance that as uncomfortable and humiliated as you are right now…it's going to get a lot worse before it gets any better. See? Doesn't that make you feel better?!

The next stage in this process was yet another return to the doctor's office, this time for a biopsy and a UUMPH (Ultimate Up-the-rear Male Personal Humiliation) procedure. Apparently everyone in the office with the possible exception of Heidi got such a bang out of the first hose insertion, that they have now decided to go for doubles, rollicking up my rear with a biopsy tube, a device previously used to bore the "Chunnel," the undersea rail tunnel from England to France, while at the very same time in an effort to break some sort of record in the Guinness Book of Medical Records they will this time also push a camera into my innards. But this time not through the backdoor. No, this time…[he swallows hard]…this time…[he swallows very hard] going up through my weewee [begins to weep softly], which is called that for the very good reason and which was quite clearly designed by God to be an exit-only, one-way drainage system. [Sobs uncontrollably] I tried to make it as clear to the doctor to the doctor as I could that I didn't think pushing a camera up my Johnson Bar would be a good idea. In fact, not at all a good idea. He said, "It's a standard procedure."

"For you maybe," I said. "But not for me and Mr. Johnson." The doctor assured me that the process would be uncomfortable but that every effort would be made to see that it was not painful. I was reminded of the old story of the young woman about to have a child who was told by her mother that childbirth is actually no more painful than pulling on her upper lip. Afterwards, when the young women confronted her mother with the obvious reality of birthing and its obvious magnitude in comparison with a pull on the lip, the mother said, "Well, actually it is like pulling your lip. Pulling your upper lip up over the top of your head…" But what must be done must be done, and those doctors' kids still needed money for books and a year abroad, so what could I do? I showed at the appointed place and the appointed time for the appointed pointing and poking, dreading the afore described lower intestine spelunkery.

First, there's that hospital gown opening to the rear. In all other cases you've probably wondered about that orientation, other than that it seems to provide no end of amusement to nurses and other bystanders. But in this case, the opening to the rear is something you better get used to because from now on most of your geezerly social contacts are going to be over your shoulder. In fact, you'll get to the point where you'll be prepared to undress and put on a rear-entry hospital gown when you step into a dentist's office. Even a barber shop. And with nary a question.

Not that it matters. At this point you will also be winding up sitting in waiting rooms with a bunch of other old guys, none of whom has the slightest notion how one sits in a dress. You are going to learn more about male comparative anatomy in the next couple months than you would have picked up if you gone to medical school. If your wife accompanies you on these visits, you better have a story ready about how you were injured in the war. God was not kind to some of us and even if you are blessed as I was by a virginal maiden like Linda who saved herself for our wedding night—that's what she says anyway—if she sits in a radiation waiting room with a bunch of old coots in hospital gowns for very long at all, she is going to come away with the experience and knowledge of comparative anatomy of a New Orleans hooker.

Anyway, no matter how much fun they might have told you or you might have thought it was going to be to have a mining machine stuffed up your rear and a camera the size of a 747 engine threaded into Mr. Happy, you're not going to laugh, no matter who tells jokes during the procedure. I didn't even see the humor when, before anything more was done than for me to lie down on the table on my side, surrounded by a mixed gender audience armed with instruments that looked like something out of a Discovery Channel special on medieval instruments of torture, the doctor said...and I am not kidding about this... "Would you like to have me position the screen so you can watch what the camera sees as we go in?"

I spent 60 years of my life observing activities in that part of my body from a distance, or not at all. I didn't make a point of staring at my winkie even when I could still see it over the abdominal horizon. Why in the name of all that's dignifying in mankind would I want a bird's eye...uh, dog's eye view of goings on down there now? And why at this point, with an audience of three doctors, two nurses, a designated finger technologist, and since I was lying there facing the wall with my butt hanging out behind me, for all I knew, a community tour of celebrity heinies? But is it really likely to a plumber that the drainpipe he is clearing is interested in knowing how the sewer snake is going to remove the clog? I don't think so. Just remove the clog and let's move on to the afterglow. So I declined the offer of a camera's eye view of the procedure. Fairly abruptly. Like "No way in hell do I want to see what the camera sees. When the DVD comes out, put me down for three copies."

For all the discomfort of the double play on my nether bits—a Salad Master™ up my wiener and a studio camera up my rear orifice, the worst part was when I was lying there like the new prisoner in cell block X, getting to know, so to speak, my new roomies, connected to machines in no way a man ever wants to be connected to anything, and I could hear the room door open. Great...just what we need...a larger audience...could it get any worse?...and of course it could and of course it did.

Now I hear a new woman's voice in the room. A young woman's voice. She expresses interest in the "procedure." I can hear her move closer and make appreciative noises about the wonderful technology being applied. Was she a doctor herself? A nurse? Someone's girlfriend who had always wanted to meet an author? No one ever said who the latest member of the audience to this drama was and I never asked. Nor by this time did I care. There were only shreds of my dignity left somewhere in my overalls' pockets anyway so there wasn't much more to lose. What the hell, lady, take a look...a good look. Any comments you'd like to make on the size of my rear end, maybe like, "Wow...I'll bet that if you knock this guy over, he bobs right back up like an inflated Bozo clown!"? Go ahead. Have at it. Or maybe "Who would have thought you could get a camera that big that far up such a little entry way? And why does this guy call it

Mr. Happy? Right now it looks to me more like Mr. Mopey—or maybe Mopey Dick. Hahahahaha"?

Am I trying to discourage you, to talk you out of such procedures, to frighten the prostate exam out of you? Not at all, my friend, not…at… all. The thing is, and what you need to keep in mind at every step of your own developing geezerhood whatever your medical affliction of choice, whatever they are doing to you, however humiliating you think it is, it's nothing compared to what they have in store of you next. See? Doesn't that make you feel better? Unlike that old joke about banging your head against a brick wall because it feels so good when you stop, now you are at the age where you really shouldn't be too discouraged about banging your head against a brick wall because that's not nearly as bad as what you're going to be banging up against that wall next. But the fact is, at some point near here you are going to conclude that from now on there is really no use in hoping that things are going to get better. Those days are over. From now on the best you can hope for is that thing don't get any worse. And that is why they call me Mr. Sunshine. At least I think that's what they call me.

You probably have guessed what happens next because this book wouldn't have much to say to you if during my next visit to the doctor he said, "You're just fine, we made a mistake reading the PSA tests, and oh by the way, Miss Nebraska Med Tech who came in to watch your biopsy says she wants me to tell you that you have a really cute heinie." No, the doctor sat Linda and me down, looked at us seriously but not with any hint of panic, and said, "The biopsy shows that you have cancer of the prostate gland."

And there is was. The C word. I had cancer. Or more precisely I guess, cancer had me. To be perfectly honest, as prepared as I was for that conclusion…for all the other things I've been called in my life I've never been known as "Lucky"… I really wasn't prepared for that conclusion. Frankly, I don't think anyone ever is. I knew when something was amiss with my heart. I had even packed my bags because I knew that I was in for a hospital stay even before I sent in to see the doctor, but I was not ready to hear the word "cancer." In fact, I didn't hear much of what the doctor said in the hour he talked with us after he said that dreaded word. (Note to oncologists: Save yourself a lot of time. The next time you tell someone they have cancer, once you say that word…"cancer"…you can pretty well save your breath and move on to your next patient. No one in that room is going to hear another word you say.)

For sixty years I had felt genuine gratitude to this old body I have been operating through my life. As I have noted a couple times previously in these pages, it served me well. It had proven durable, serviceable, user-friendly, generally well constructed for the purposes to which it was intended. I had begun to sense some wear and tear here and there, to be sure, but that was to be expected. I had worn out or broken some small parts but by and large they had either self-repaired or were easily tacked together with duct tape and baling wire, as is proper.

Maybe that's the thing with cancer…it isn't your own mechanisms starting to wear out or letting you down; while they are your own cells doing you dirt, the impression is that cancer is an alien invasion, with the good ol' body you've come to love and appreciate having to fight off a genuinely ferocious and obnoxious invader, an unseen and insidious saboteur who wants to bring the whole thing crashing down. Perhaps our enormous trauma upon hearing the word "cancer" is because we pretty much all know by now that as horrendous as the assault is on our bodies by this ugly, uninvited betrayer in our midst is, the ferocity of the war you are going to wage against the demon in your own body in trying to get rid of it is liable to take a fairly ferocious toll on the landscape around it, which is to say, you.

The strategy for that war is the next step. Okay, I have cancer. Once I got used to that idea, what's next? What do we do to stop it from doing any more damage than it has already done? And while we're at it, how much damage has it done up to this point? Well, let's face it, even the good news in this situation is going to be bad news, but there is bad news, worse news, and… well…the worst news. And you find that you take comfort where you can. Yes, I had cancer. And yes, it should be treated. But no, it had not spread beyond the prostate gland…which would have been the worse news. And apparently the worst case scenario, expansion of the disease to other organs or the lymph system, had not yet happened. Whew. Okay. That may not be exactly what I would call great news but right now I was grasping for straws. And I certainly didn't want to get cocky at this point because not only could the cancer still spread, the very procedures we had done so far…the biopsy, the colonoscopy, the wieneroscopy…might be precisely the disturbance provoking the cancer to migrate, another case of the cure being simply more of the danger.

We met with the oncologist and he told us what I was in store for, and it was not something to anticipate with any glee. At least we had time to think about what course we would chose to take. And please do know that at this point what I am trying to do by telling you all this about my own experiences is not to gain your sympathy…my experiences are little more than typical and if anything at all less dramatic than those of millions of others. Nor am I suggesting my decisions were the right ones, or that you should do what I did, or not do what I did, or even that you will have to deal with prostate cancer. In all seriousness, what I want you to learn from my experiences, even if I can make you chuckle now and again, is that as you grow older, you are going to face some afflictions and decisions, some prognoses, diagnoses, and treatments of your own. Some triumphs and some disappointments. My intentions here are to tell you that you are anything but alone, that you can still laugh through all this, that you pretty much have to do what you have to do, that whatever the pain or discomfort involved in the problem or its cure…you're going to survive. Or you're not. All you can do is what you can do, so you might as well do it and make the best of it as you can. I hope that's not discouraging to you. It wasn't to me and I sure don't mean it to be for you. I am an old grump (Linda often reminds me) but I like to think I am not a chronic whiner. Even when things have looked pretty bleak for me, I still enjoyed a warm afternoon in the sun scratching my dogs' ears, I have still found pleasure in a good book (reading one or writing one), I have always had the love of my family and friends, I have still found reason to laugh and love myself. I'm no Pollyanna…in fact, I have a reputation for being something of a grouch, a recognition I consider to be an inherent privilege of geezerhood. But I am practical: there's no use spending a lot of energy grumping about something you either can't do anything about or are doing everything you…and others…can do.

The reason I inject that moment of seriousness in this volume that I otherwise hope will be a matter of good cheer for the reader is that this step, the first visit with the doctor, about any major medical consequence of Geezerhood, is pretty much the worst part of the whole process. It's not that doctors are particularly insensitive (although some are) but because in order to protect themselves and to prepare you, they have to give you the whole load of potential woe, the entire list of possibly disastrous consequences, every miserable, lurid detail, the worst case scenario, the most dire of outcomes, a crushing catalog of every potential side effect anyone anywhere has ever suffered who has gone through this same course of treatment, even if it is only one exception within a million other happy examples. And in cases such as cancer, those unhappy potentials are not only the painful results of the disease but also of the possible cure for it.

Now, if I may offer just a word of encouragement, please do try to keep in mind that the chances are good that you are not going to suffer all of the worst effects in the list of either the disease or the cure. In fact, far from it. You may suffer only a few of the possible side effects. And even then what you experience by way of possible collateral damage of the cure may be on the luckily less pernicious side of the balance sheet. Hopefully, you won't have any of the worst side effects, only a few of the milder ones, and even then, whatever they happen to be, that they will be of the very minimum seriousness.

The doctor sat down with us for more than an hour, showed us a video about prostate cancer and treatments, then talked with us at great length and in careful detail about all of the problems of the disease and of the possible courses we would now be called upon to decide. Just hearing about the treatments is unpleasant enough; as you listen to the endless list of horrendous consequences… clogged urinary tracts that can be cleared only with medical grade sewer snakes, destroyed lower digestive tracts and the need for optional exit vents for waste products (eeeeeeuuuuuuuw!), loss of hair, exhaustion, nausea, impotence, burns, irritation, diarrhea, constipation, and the unsettling percentage of men who go through all this and still are not cured…. At several points I know I turned green and I had to tell the doctor that I really had heard enough. I didn't want to hear anything more about what could go wrong. I was prepared to accept treatment, so couldn't we skip the horror stories?

No, we can't. It's not a matter of going through the motions. I once bought a water softener for my home and I knew that I wanted to buy a water softener. I also knew that water softener salesmen have a magic act they go through when pitching their product where they take a glass of your tap water, add chemicals, and show you how rocks, and wiggly things, and enough gravel to finish your driveway settle out of your water. I told the softener salesman who came to our house with a contract and a samples case containing the props for his magic act that I didn't need the show, that I was ready to sign and buy the water conditioner…but no kidding, this guy couldn't bring himself to proceed without doing the entire routine. He didn't know how to sell a water softener without the magic show. But, as I told him, I didn't want to see the magic show. Give me the paper, here's the check, deliver and install the softener as soon as you can. Nope, he couldn't do it. He simply had to go through his performance; after all, it was as close as he'd ever get to show business. So I sat my three toddler kids on the couch, the salesman set up his show, and he amazed and traumatized them by demonstrating how rocks and gravel, rhinoceros skeletons, and junked automobiles settle out of our tap water when his magic potions were added to it.

That's not the way it works in the medical world. It's no magic act. It's no sales pitch. You <u>do</u> need to know what the potential consequences are of your medical decisions... <u>all</u> the potential consequences. But you also have to keep in mind that while you are reviewing the entire inventory of potential consequences of any treatment, there is a high probability that you will experience only a small portion of those negative effects, hopefully in less than the highest intensity of their worst degree. It won't be easy to keep all that good and common sense in mind while the doctor sits there in front of you scaring the bejeezus out of you but keep telling yourself, "Self, stay calm...it ain't gonna be this bad...it ain't gonna be this bad...it ain't gonna be this bad. And even if it is, we can get through this just as we've gotten through everything else we've had to get through up to this point."

On the other hand, you are going to have to make some hard decisions. While a doctor may make suggestions, even recommendations about the best course of treatment, inevitably you are going to have to make some choices. This is not a medical primer, and frankly I don't know what I'm talking about, but in my case, with prostate cancer, the options presented to me were roughly

1.  Don't do anything...everyone gets prostate cancer... men at least... you may have it and not even know it...if you are old already the problems and consequences of the treatment may be worse than whatever problems you may have from the cancer itself;

2.  Remove the prostate gland... a pretty drastic course of action because it is enormously invasive on your poor body that has already been abused by the cancer, and while surgical removal of the entire prostate gland certainly takes care of the problem, it can have some drastic side effects too—for example, some recovery time in the hospital...always a dangerous place to be...

3. Plant radiation "seeds" or pellets in the prostate so that the radiation works on the cancer over a period of time. A short time in the hospital is required for this procedure. Hopefully the radiation will eventually kill off the cancer... again, this is a fairly invasive procedure but not as bad as surgery. On the other hand, it is more drastic than the fourth alternative, which is...

4. External radiation, which is invasive only in that it requires frequent visits to the clinic—daily for months-- with enormously uncomfortable inserts of a balloon device up your...oh, no, here it is again...up your you- know-where. (It's always your butt, isn't it? Who would have thought that your ass would be so versatile?!)

The doctor told us we would have a few months to decide what we wanted to do from the above menu, during which time we would start treatment with me getting a series of enormously expensive Lupron shots to reduce the hormones that feed prostate cancer, thus putting it on hold until we geared up to attack it more vigorously. And...uh... oh yeah...of course that will have its side effects too, he mentioned casually. Aside from the major damage the shots would do to our bank balance, they would, uh, sort of, in a way...help me understand Linda more as she approaches menopause because, er, well... the shots would let me enjoy all the benefits of that process otherwise monopolized by women. Yes, the Lupron shots would enable me to...go through all the symptoms of menopause—including hot flashes and night sweats.

Well, hunkydamndory. Now I'm going to show all the symptoms of the precise female estrogen that I've always made so much fun of. The doctor was telling me that I was going to be in touch with my feminine side now, like it or not. And that wasn't going to be just another psychobabble metaphor.

Upon hearing that news, Linda said, "Oh boy, Rog...now maybe we can look at paint samples together." That sure helped my disposition. The doctor said that other side effects might be that I could be confused, irritable, and forgetful. Terrific...now there was apparently a chance I would wind up voting Republican! Linda offered to loan me her t-shirt that said TOMORROW I'M 51 AND ALL I GOT WAS THIS LOUSY HOT FLASH. He also said that I might have some loss of hair, but only in the affected area... which would be...my butt. Since I am anything but hirsute- challenged in that area of my body, I responded that if that particular problem arose I would simply do what most men do--go for a comb-over.

Things were getting ugly and it was clear that I was going to have to strike back...both at the problems that came along with this stage of the treatment and everyone who seemed intent on giving me a bad time about them. I settled on several strategies. First, if a buddy started kidding me about the Lupron shots and my new menopausal self, I would say, "Look, the side effects of this drug are drastically overstated, a way the medical system can protect itself from adverse legal consequences. The doctors tell you everything that could <u>possibly</u> go wrong even though any one patient will actually experience very few, if any of them. The term 'menopause' is only used as a form of shorthand, not as a precise description of what is actually happening. In fact, so far I have yet to feel even the slightest effects of the Lupron, yet anything approaching what I understand to be symptoms of female menopause. I appreciate your concern but [beginning to sob] there's NOTHING WRONG WITH ME! WOULD YOU PLEASE LEAVE ME ALONE AND STOP PICKING ON ME! WHY ARE YOU BEING SO MEAN TO ME?! AND WHY DON'T WE JUST CUDDLE ANYMORE?

NOW...GIVE ME YOUR CREDIT CARD...I'M GOING SHOPPING UNTIL I FEEL BETTER! [COLLAPSES IN UNCONTROLLABLE HYSTERIA]

I found that one performance like that, especially in any public place, usually headed off any further joking about new developments in my physical and mental state. Beyond that, I simply accepted the problems like the hot flashes and night sweats as minor and temporary problems hopefully leading toward later and more important results. Besides, that winter we really cut back on our heating bills.

As uncomfortable as the Lupron anti-hormone shots made me, I knew I was still facing the more drastic procedures of the radiation treatments. I wasn't so much worried about the radiation and the long list of possible side effects as I was the process itself. Please note that what I am about to tell you now is not going to be pleasant for you to read, so imagine what it would be like if it were done to you. And if you are a man, there are good chances that as you yourself approach Geezerhood, you may very well face that prospect. (Oh, by the way, women as a rule don't suffer from prostate problems.) One of the direct results of our wonderfully increased longevity is that we are all the more likely to wind up with the consequences of being older…one of which is prostate and other cancers.

Okay…here it goes. I am going to tell you in some detail about the radiation treatments I underwent for prostate cancer. (For obvious reasons, the names of the people involved have been changed to protect the guilty, and not incidentally to protect me from angry husbands since I will be speaking of some fairly intimate moments I had with their wives.) I don't even want to talk about this, and I know you're not going to want to hear about it, but hey, that's what this book is about. So…brace yourself.

The thing is, radiology techies (that's what us medical professionals call technologists) are going to place you very precisely on a sliding table under a huge humming gantry and then precisely aim a beam of radiation at a very small specific spot of your innards and then very briefly zap you. The theory is that cancer cells don't recover from radiation burns as quickly or well as healthy cells do, so every day for weeks they are going to slightly singe your prostate <u>inside of you</u> and then let you heal overnight, or over weekends. Your internal healthy cells are burned and they struggle mightily to recover; the cancer cells are equally burned, but don't do so well with the upswing. Over time then, hopefully, the cancer cells finally give up and quit, leaving the field of cellular combat to the healthy cells. But that's not the worst part.

Of course with radiation treatments you are dealing with internal burns (there's not much sign of the burns on your outside other than minor irritation like a rash on the skin near the area where the radiation rays go into your body), even though they are small, and your body suffers for that. And it is never convenient to go into a clinic for daily (or thereabouts) treatments, especially out here in the boondocks. Others have to make much longer trips, even involving overnight stays in the city where the clinic is located. The bottom line is, when you are taking radiation treatments, you can pretty much count on your days being shot for a couple of months. But that's not the worst part.

The worst part is, seriously, the indignation of it all. At least for us gents who have that little extra part exclusive to our gender, the prostate. The prostate is deep down in there somewhere, and it's close to other vitals like your urinary tract, lower intestine, etc., so accurate aiming of that zapper beam is pretty damned important. But the prostate can move around a little inside you (I was told) and so it needs to be stabilized when you are lying there on a table under the zapper beam machine (also called an "accelerator") covered by nothing but a sheet. But that is definitely not the worst part.

Hmmm…how can we stabilize something—that being his prostate gland-- way inside of him? Hey, I've got it! How about we shove a hose with a balloon on the end of it up his rear end to the area right next to the prostate, inflate the balloon, and let the balloon push the prostate and hold it steady for the radiation beam?! And gents, that is precisely what they do. I got queasy just listening to the oncologist describe the process. A balloon up my butt? Which is then inflated? You're kidding, right? Let me guess…the techies wear clown outfits and before insertion they tie the balloon into the shape of a dachshund or giraffe just for fun? Every day for ten weeks… do I have that right? And the person doing the honors will be…that incredibly attractive woman standing right over there… As if I hadn't had quite enough humiliation from attractive women when I was in high school, and then when I was in college, and then from my first wife, and then a whole series of women when I was again single...now...I am going to suffer the most incredible of indignities again and again and again...fifty times, in fact... from a team of lovely ladies whose names I don't even know yet, and who have access to my nether regions and various tools of torture...for which I will then pay a fortune. This can't be the real world. I'm dreaming, right?

The rad tech who gave me my preliminary tour of the facility and briefed me on what I would be going through for next few months tried to reassure me by telling me that by the time the treatments were over, I would consider the rad techs to be my friends and actually miss them when the series of treatments was over. Yeah, right! Like that is going to happen! I'm going to come to miss daily humiliations and assaults on parts of my body that for the past 60 years have been fairly private property. I'll miss these butt-balloon stuffing ladies when I miss the cancer itself!

As the time approached for my first treatment and my anxiety about baring my heinie for the first balloon ascension rose, I finally admitted my growing fear and anguish about this humiliating procedure to my good friend Dick. For all my joking, for all my gratitude that there is after all something that can be done about this affliction that for all of man's history had simply been another way to die, I was filled with the dread of facing those ladies with their hose and balloon...or, to be more precise, not facing them since they would be approaching me for the occasions in a flanking movement, as it were. God, how was I going to bear this insult to my pride once, yet fifty times. And the indignity was going to be all the worse because this humiliation was going to be inflicted on me by women... Or did that element make the whole thing more humiliating? Hmmmm... Would I really want some guy doing this same thing? No, I guess not. And wasn't the embarrassment going to be even worse because these were really very attractive women...no, it wasn't...but would it

really have been better if they were ugly hags...no, it wouldn't...
Oh God, I was filled with the horror of the anticipation. Would I
be able to actually go through this radiation thing when the time
comes? And not just once...but <u>fifty times</u>! Day after day...a
humiliation that shouldn't happen to any man once...and it was
about to become my daily routine. How was I going to bear this?
Could I bear it?

And at that moment Dick saved my life. He said the perfect
thing, the Ultimate Truth that swept away the fog of fear in my
mind. "Rog," he said, "look at it this way...to those women,
you're just another asshole."

And you know, that's a pretty good summary of exactly what
was going on. To them I <u>was</u> just another asshole. I don't know if
it's part of radiation technologist training but the ladies who went
every day where few had gone before achieved and delivered a
remarkable balance between treating me compassionately as a
human being who was thoroughly embarrassed by this whole
thing (as it were) and yet maintaining a professional detachment
that eventually brought things to the point where we could talk
and even joke even as one of them pushed or pulled a hose up my
rear end and inflated the balloon on the end. I know it sounds
utterly unlikely but that is, no kidding, precisely what happened,
and actually fairly early in the process. Damned if by the end of
the ten weeks and I left after my final treatment...precisely as the
lady had told me, I did consider them my friends...and I knew
that I would indeed miss them. I told them in fact that I hoped I
would meet them again somewhere in our movements around the
same town...maybe in a restaurant or grocery store, realizing of
course that they might only recognize me from behind. And that
I'd just as soon not want to buy the tomato—or chocolate
doughnut-- they had just picked up and checked for firmness
unless I could be sure if they'd washed their hands recently.

Despite the discomfort of the procedure, the mood in the
radiation room quickly lightened and soon jokes were far more
common a commodity than complaints. Doug, the medical
"architect" who designed the cushions they would be using to

hold me solid and immobile on the radiation table the next three months was present during the rehearsal run-throughs to get everything set by way of establishing aiming points for the radiation beams. After Sweet Carla had inserted the balloon hose, taken her calculations regarding exactly how far up my…uh…disposition it had to go to hold the prostate, Doug helpfully said I would have the option of Carla deflating the balloon before pulling it out or removing it as is. I opined that I sure didn't want her letting the air suddenly out of the inserted balloon if it meant I was going to fly insanely around the room when she let it loose as released balloons tend to do.

After establishing exactly the angle and approach of the radiation beams from the accelerator, three points of reference had to be established and marked on me so laser beams could be set to triangulate my exact position under the radiation gantry. There couldn't be any room for mistake at this stage of the process. You want that beam aimed precisely every time, so the three marks they used to aim had to be located with pinpoint accuracy…and permanently. You sure didn't want marks that would wash off the first time you stepped into a shower! So Sweet Carla graciously gave me three free tattoos as a part of my initiation to the world of radiation treatment…three small but permanent dots, one on each thigh and one on my lower stomach, just north of Mr. Happy. On my next visit I told RadTech Carla that I'd been collecting free drinks at biker bars showing off my new tattoos, but I pretty much reserved for close male friends my boast that when Mr. Happy really got happy, if you catch my drift, the tattoo low and dead center on my frontal exposure expanded to read WELCOME TO NEBRASKA! DRIVE CAREFULLY AND COME BACK TO VISIT US SOON AGAIN!

Carla had already seen too much of my physical endowments, or lack therefore, to take that smart-aleck line at all seriously. When I complained to the rad techs that it seemed kind of silly to have nothing more than small dots as orientation points, that as long as they were going to install tattoos they might just as well have done something more spectacular by way of the triangulation tattoos…you know, maybe something saying MOM or BORN FREE, it was Techie Melanie who suggested that one on my rear hip could have said something useful like EXIT ONLY. I wound up opting for tattoos saying CAUTION—I MAKE WIDE RIGHT TURNS on my right hip and WIDE LOAD—PASS CAREFULLY; IF YOU CAN'T SEE MY MIRRORS I CAN'T SEE YOU on the left hip.

The treatment was that I would show up at the clinic every day, change into a hospital gown, and take a seat in the waiting room until they were ready for me in the radiation room. At only our second or third visit we learned something interesting when Linda tore a coupon out of the waiting room newspaper. I mean, you know, no one else was there. It's not like she was stealing. And besides, since no one could see her…and then the announcement came over a speaker that they were ready for me. They had seen that I was there over the monitoring camera in the waiting room…which meant…they also had the goods on Linda, a.k.a., Ms. Coupon Lightfinger. The next day Doug came into the waiting room and told us that all medical offices in a five-county area had been alerted about Linda and her coupon snitching days were over. That day my humiliation in having Lovely Carla push a balloon up my rear was nothing to Linda's klepto-humiliation.

Anyway, when called I would go back to the radiation room and lie on the table. The ladies would daintily lift my flimsy covering and redrape me with a bit of cloth that always seemed inadequate to the task. Not that it mattered—the task they faced made the formality of the cover only that. Each and every day they were pretty much going to extinguish any pretense I might have had to modesty or dignity. (That is the ultimate lesson of geezerhood—Abandon hope all ye who enter here, or perhaps more precisely, all ye who are entered here.)

The first step of the daily treatment was an ultra-sound examination to determine where my prostate might have wandered within my innards overnight. One of the lovelies in attendance would warn, "Okay, Rog, warm goo…" and smear my stomach with something unsettlingly erotic. I mean, jeez, as I explained to Linda, I was now helpless—flat on my back, lying under a huge gantry device, unable to move, completely at the mercy of these women who were free to indulge in their every kinky fantasy. I mean, man…dimmed lights, warm goo, my choice of music (classical rock and roll), naked, two attractive women attending to my every comfort, soft voices, warm hands, long, cool fingers… The ultrasound device was rolled around on my lower stomach until the ladies found whatever it was they were looking for, or not looking for…how would I know?… I could only hope that one of the days they were doing this sonar examination of my innards they wouldn't announce, "Contratulations, Rog…it's a boy!"

All of this was just fine and dandy (although maybe not quite as erotic as I am making it sound in retrospect, I'll have to admit) but then came the real mood breaker. While I pretended to be oblivious to all the above, one of the techies inserted the balloon hose up my kiester and inflated it, and then I would try to lie perfectly still while one or two of these fairly petite ladies pushed and shoved and tugged on the cloth on which I was lying to position me precisely for the beam by lining up three lasers built into the zapper machine with the three tattoos with which Sweet Carla had decorated me. I'm one big boy and so it was some kind of job for these two women, the two together half my weight, to move my dead weight around. One day, trying to make light of their labors, I commented that after a couple months or so moving me around on that radiation machine they would be ready to take a job over at the onion factor throwing around hundred pound bags of onions.

Whereupon began a conversation between them of their amazement that anyone could possibly work with the constant smell of onions. Now, these were ladies who had just moments before…. Well, I had to laugh out loud at the thought of a couple women over at the onion factory throwing around sacks of onions and commenting about how they couldn't imagine their neighbor

Carla working at the cancer clinic on hose-and-balloon duty... I guess it's all relative.

There were three women who carried the burden of the balloon work. At first I couldn't tell if they were married...one doesn't wear a wedding ring in their line of work, I guess. Along the way I did get some hints about their marital status simply by things that were said. For example, at one point I was in the gantry about ready to start treatment, my balloon firmly in place, when one of the techies tried to talk with me over the hum of the accelerator. I'm hard of hearing anyway but sometimes if I can see who is talking I can better follow a conversation, so I said to whoever it was, "You know, it would be easier for me to know what you're saying if I could see who is talking. Maybe you should put a mirror here under the gantry so the patient can see who's saying what." I think it was Carla who said, "Yeah sure...my husband isn't all that happy with my line of work as it is, and you want me to put mirrors on the ceiling!"

On another occasion the two ladies installing and inflating the balloon were talking about a party they were having that weekend and I decided that if anyone knows how to have a good time on weekends, it would have to be radiation technologists, considering what they had been doing all week and realizing that pretty much nothing would remain sacred or off limits for those lovely ladies! And I can only imagine what kind of nicknames they must have for each of their patients. I'm not sure I want to know what mine would be.

But I've gotten a little ahead of myself. Let's take a couple steps back. Without question the most memorable moment during the treatments, the one I would recount a thousand times to anyone who would listen, was early in the series. I came into the radiation room, still pretty discouraged and embarrassed by the whole process, only to find that the lady with the hose and balloon in her hand on this occasion was not one of the ones I had met in the half dozen previously visits but a woman of absolutely stunning beauty--Carla. Every rad techie I met (with the notable exception of Dougie) was an attractive woman, so when I say this one was stunning, I mean she was flat-out gorgeous. And there I was, lying on her table, next to naked, and she was about to put warm goo on my stomach to take a sonogram verifying the location of my prostate and then…shove a hose up my rear. Gulp. If you think I am exaggerating her attractiveness, late in my treatments an old friend Russ was visiting from Oregon and took the chance for conversation to drive me to the city for my treatment one day. As I exited and he saw Lovely Carla , Russ sat there slack jawed and glassy eyed and expressed his interest in showing his compassion for my discomforture by stepping back to the radiation room with Carla for a sample radiation treatment of his own, just for the fun of it. Carla is that gorgeous.

I know what you're thinking…this is way too much. Well, you're going to have to hear more because there was a lot more that day and things got substantially worse, or better, depending on how you feel about such things. As it turns out, there are several, uh, approaches to your nether port, and I don't know whether they learn the different styles at different schools or whether it's a matter of personal preference, but different techies approach the landing field, as it were, under different modes of instrumentation. Techie Cheryline would have me lift the knee of my right leg and do a kind of over-under approach. Melanie announced without ado "Assume the froggie position!" which meant that I was to lift both legs into the air to provide her with some working room…not at all a stance that offers a fellow much hope of dignity, I can tell you for a fact. But now here I am, awaiting instructions from this vision of beauty. She says…and I am <u>not</u> kidding here… "Okay, Rog, I do this a little differently than some of the other girls, so just humor me. Relax. Put your right leg over my left shoulder. Now, put your left leg over my right shoulder."

Gulp. Try to imagine my astonishment at this moment. When was the last time you heard those words from the mouth of a beautiful woman? Or an ugly woman, for that matter. I'd been waiting for this invitation all my life but this would have been the last place in the world I would have expected it. "Shouldn't you at least buy me a glass of wine first?" I sputtered, totally nonplussed for one of the few times in my life. And only when the treatment was over that day did she say, "Oh, by the way, my name is Carla."

"Look," I said, "I'm sure not one to tell you your business but I really think you should make a point of introducing yourself earlier in this procedure before setting up any other prostate patients for this sort of radiation treatment. I've had to make a life commitment to women for less intimacy than you and I just had, and I didn't even know your name!"

Small wonder that Carla became something of a favorite of mine even though she severely limited my ability to elicit for the sympathy from my friends and family. God knows, Russ never again felt sorry for me during my period of radiation treatments.

The only real problem during the series of radiation treatments arose immediately following my very last treatment. The radiation technologists have a little ritual "graduation" for whoever completes a treatment series-- a small gift, a bit of a song, and kind wishes for recovery. Linda was invited to come back to the treatment area from the waiting room to share in this moment of real joy…the end of a long and grueling process. As we left the building and walked to Linda's car, she said, "Uh, who was the really attractive woman with the dark hair?"

Uh-oh. Not even cancer was going to make this one easy to explain because I had already laughed with Linda about Carla's approach, as it were, to anal balloon insertion. "Oh, that's… uh… Carla," I mumbled, hoping Linda might not remember my gushing about Carla's bedside manner and that the whole issue would just blow over quickly. And so it seemed to do. "Oh…Carla …" she said. But then a more thoughtful "Oh…. Carla !" And then she stopped walking. This wasn't going to be a pretty scene, I could tell. "CARLA ?" Linda sputtered. "You mean 'just put your right leg over my left shoulder' Carla ?!"

And thus endeth the sympathy on the home front, the moral of the story being that however uncomfortable you might be from radiation treatments, no matter how tired or even as sick you get day to day, day after day, there may be some advantages for you to drive yourself to the clinic. At least if your radiation techie is Lovely Carla. I probably won't have to worry myself about that problem in the future if I ever have to go back for more radiation: Linda says if there are any further treatments, it'll be Doug doing the ballooning honors.

Seeking sympathy, I had told just about everyone I know about my balloon stuffing treatments…in part certainly because I enjoyed the look of complete horror on their faces and the inevitable reaction, "And then…she <u>inflates</u> it?!" And for a while I increased my mileage on that element of the treatment by buying a small sack of children's balloons and sending them out to friends with a note saying something like, "No sense in this nice balloon going to waste, right? And it's almost like new…trust me, it was only used once!"

I had a lot of fun with that gag until my pal Paul Jensen got a couple of my balloons in the mail and e-mailed tersely back, "Funny…from everything I've heard about you, I expected the balloons to be much larger." End of balloon gags. Now the smart lines were starting to come back and bite <u>me</u>!

During the weeks of radiation treatment the Monday ritual varied a bit because on those days I would go to the lab for a blood letting, a process I absolutely abhor. I cut myself with Dracula-like regularity when I am working in my shop and come back to the house at the end of the day with my socks, shirt, or hair soaked in blood…"didn't have time to stop"…"it's nothing"…"don't worry." But when a phlebotomist at a medical lab goes into my arm with that railroad spike needle he saves especially for me and digs around trying to corner one of my "rolling veins," I turn green and look for a soft spot on the floor for my impending landing.

Mondays were also the day I would have a visit with the oncologist about how things were going. To my delight I was able to report at every step along the way that almost none of the side effects he had warned me about were showing up. That is, considering everything I was going through, I was doing pretty well. Now, you have to know that even though I was going to a "city" clinic...our nearest community of any size is still only 50,000 but out here in the middle of the sticks that is what passes for a city, so.... But our doctors are not, in my experience, city doctors in the usual sense of that concept. For example, this particular doctor, the oncologist, had made it very clear that I shouldn't miss any treatments unless absolutely necessary and unless I cleared it with him. No sense in letting those cancer cells recover any more than we could help, he explained. But, I worried, what if in the later weeks of the series, when we were in a time of the year when ferocious blizzards can blast the Plains, I couldn't even get out of my driveway yet to the clinic for my daily treatment. My farm is on a highway but it is not a heavily traveled route and no matter what else is taken into account, we are out here in the Middle of Nowhere. "Easy enough," he said. "My farm is only eight miles from yours, so if you have trouble getting out of your place, I'll just come over with my huge all-wheel drive urban assault vehicle and get you!" Now, that's a house call in spades!

The oncologist gave me other reasons to trust him too. For one thing, he didn't try to flimflam me with fancy medical language or phony airs. At one point I asked him about the special diet he had outlined for me...was it to speed the treatment? To ease the effects of the disease? Or to avoid me being any sicker from the radiation than necessary? I wanted to know because no matter how much I fudged on my diet, it didn't seem to make much difference. So...what was the purpose of the special list of foods I was to observe?

He mused a moment...I could tell he was searching for just the right words, a technical formulation that would speak to my own advanced education and sophisticated ways. "You should watch what you eat...because..." he said, pausing again, "you don't want to have to spend all day sitting on the shitter." That was language and reasoning I could understand. I thanked him and praised him for his technical knowledge. "Yeah," he said, "you might just as well go ahead and eat what you want."

"Great," I said. "Now I won't have to be as careful as I have been...like yesterday when I had three chili dogs for lunch and sauerkraut pizza for supper." "Right," he said. "No sense in overdoing that moderation thing."

He is also the only doctor to this day I have ever heard use the terms "Johnson bar" and "T'ain't" when referring to human anatomy. If you know what those terms refer to, then you realize what a gem of a doctor this is. If you don't know those terms..., well, I guess any doctor will do. Early on I asked this doctor about whether or not I could drink beer during my radiation treatments. "Not more than a case at a time," he advised. But my favorite was the time he asked if there was anything he could do to make my life easier now that I was well along in the treatments. "Well, yes," I said. "You could sure set my mind at ease if you would write to the Jack Daniels people and ask them why the hell they lowered the proof of their whiskey without so much as letting anyone know, yet lowering the price." As soon as I got the news about them watering down the whiskey I had dashed to the local market and sorted through their shelf stock, culling out and grabbing up all the authentic proof whiskey and leaving the watered down stuff sitting there for someone else to use as drain cleanser. "I would like to get influential people like you," I told the doctor, "to write to the Jack Daniels distillery and let them know we feel cheated."

"Roger," the doctor said sternly. "You're drinking Jack Daniels?! You shouldn't be drinking Jack Daniels anyway." Uh-oh. Had I fritzed my treatment protocol? Was I killing myself? "No," he said sternly. "You should be drinking...Makers Mark! And they are having a sale on it right now over at Sun Mart...even cheaper than the black label swill!" And he proceeded to give me a lecture on how bad booze makes for bad health while good booze is like a magic elixir. I turned to Linda and pronounced in glee, "A doctor is telling me that I should be drinking a better brand of whiskey! Linda, he says I should be drinking Maker's Mark. This is as good as a prescription!" And Linda being the woman I married and love drove me directly from the cancer clinic to Sun Mart to...er...fill my new prescription. Every doctor should be so thoughtful. (The same doctor says he learned everything he knows about this nectar from his mother, who refers to it as "Magic Marker!")

As the radiation treatments progressed, it was clear that I was obviously slowing down physically. Constant internal damage, even if kept to a minimum, is still something of a physical insult to the body, after all. Even more wearing was the enormous five or six hour gouge taken out of every day by our preparations to drive to the clinic for the treatment, the actual time and effort of driving there, taking the treatment, sometimes getting blood taken or talking with the doctor, driving home, resting up, and then... well, then doing what I could with what little time and energy I had left. As I fell further and further behind in my work, it did start to grind on my disposition, I'll have to admit.

As I like to point out, I won't even eat irradiated meat, and now I <u>was</u> one! I made lame jokes about now being able to warm up left-over pizza simply by holding the plate on my lap a few minutes. I bragged that Linda was now having an easier time finding me in the dark because certain parts of me glowed in the dark, but even the novelty of that amusement began to fade when at bed time she took to singing "Glow, Little Glow Worm, Glimmer! Glimmer!"

But my spirit returned when the best line of my entire cancer experience was delivered out of nowhere, apparently without effort, by my favorite local wit, Good Ol' Eric. I encountered him one day on Main Street in town and he asked me what was new. I told him well, damn, I had prostate cancer. His face suddenly went serious and he said, "Man, there are going to be a lot of unhappy people here in town when that word gets around. [Dramatic pause] Most of the money in the pool at the tavern is on your liver..." That one punch line made the whole misery I was enduring worthwhile. I love laughter, and so despite the looming possibility of death and suffering...for me, of all people!...the ability of my friends, the doctors, Linda, the nurses, and the technologists to laugh...with me and at me...was the saving grace for what could have been only a long, miserable period of fear and pain.

When the radiation treatments were finished I began the long, slow road to regaining my strength, taken from me not as much by cancer or even the treatment as the long period of relative inactivity the treatments had imposed on me. Even if I had the strength to get some physical activity into my day, there wasn't any time left for anything after everything to took to prepare for radiation, get to radiation, have the radiation, return from radiation, and recovery from all that.

Linda said she could sense however that the manhood stolen by the Lupron shots was returning when I again became inconsiderate, messy, and lazy and my humor resumed the junior high school level of the normal American male. As for myself, I was just glad the radiation treatments ended before winter set in. As fond as I had become of the Lovely Ladies of Radiation Technology and their fetching manner, not mention their long, slender, gentle, cool fingers, I knew from experience that if things had gone on much past the first frost I would have had to spend a fortune buying them all hand warmers. Linda surely would have begun to suspect.

As I write these narratives, I wonder what some of you must be thinking. How can I say such outrageous things about other women when my lovely wife Linda, whom I adore, is going to see all this sooner or later. Well, take it from me, Linda is perfectly capable of taking care of herself. And anyone else. Her razor wit makes sure I get away with absolutely nothing at all without suitable punishment. After all, she's Catholic.

But if you need further evidence of Linda's complete control of this and every other situation, skip a few pages to the stories below about my birthday fantasy of a bedly threesome or the tale about the time my female television producer screamed out my name in burning passion when her husband came home late and crawled into her bed in the middle of the night. Believe me, my comments about other women are all idle chatter and any moment whatsoever Linda wants to shorten the leash and restrict the Old Dog's mental wanderings, she can do it with only the slightest flick of her wrist. Or lash of her tongue.

Fair warning—even after radiation treatments end, there is a regimen that needs to be followed for another year or so to avoid further dire consequences. So to this day Linda mixes up a "glass of sunshine" (Citrucel) for me for happy hour every late afternoon and we keep a supply of "magic bullets" (glycerin suppositories) on hand just in case. Just today I asked the doctor if I couldn't simplify the process and make it a damn site more convenient by just swallowing them since eventually they make their way to the targeted area anyway. My father hated suppositories as much as I do. He always said that they taste terrible and for all the good they did him he might just as well have gone ahead and stuffed them up his butt. My doctor said he had never thought of or tried the oral approach but he did know that had learned from the experience of some of his medically uninitiated patients that he makes a point of telling guys like me that before, uh, using suppositories, whichever way you chose to get them into your body, you need to take the foil wrapper off. Good advice. And ouch.

# LIFESTYLES OR MAYBE NOT:

Even when the problems of ageing are not precise clinical malfunctions for which there are cures but simply a normal part of the process, they lead nonetheless to distress and adjustment. After all, this is almost certainly the first time you've gotten old, right? I can tell you for a fact this is the first time for me. And so we don't have a lot of experience at this. Even if we've read about it, seen it happen, or laughed at it in cartoon strips or movies, we still don't really understand what it's like to get old and probably haven't even thought it was going to happen to us. And yet suddenly…or at least it seems that it is suddenly…here it is: We're Geezers.

And adjust you will, will ye nor nill ye, as Shakespeare would put it. And as with everything else, like the Lovely Carla magically appearing as my Balloon Angel, there can be an upside to it all if you only look for it and appreciate it. For example, once you sense that time is growing short and that you are not immortal as you had hoped and somehow believed all along, you will as I have mentioned above assume a mode all humans should have through their lives of not tolerating stupid, unpleasant, annoying, or simply unlikable people. You will realize somewhere along the point where you enter those hahahahahahahaha Golden Years that you don't have nearly enough time for the people you love, so there really isn't much sense in tolerating people you don't like. Or even people you do like but who get in the way of spending more time with people you love. If there is such a stage of life as the "Fix-It Fifties," there is also an even more satisfying era of "Give-A-Shit Sixties." And maybe the "Seditious Seventies."

Along this same line, you will eventually make the enormous decision that now is the time, that this is that special occasion you've been saving everything for. For me it was a bottle of French Calvados brandy I had tucked away in my potations cellar for "a special occasion." I think it was somewhere between my two cardiac "events" and the bout with cancer that I realized that the most likely scenario if things continued the way they were going, was that my buddies were going to open that bottle and drink it over my coffin. Knowing their miserable tastes in drink, they would probably stir a shot or two of this wonderful stuff into whiskey sour mix and then pour the rest out onto the ground because it had obviously gone bad over the years, not being nearly as good as a sour with Kesslers. My secret wish now that I've turned the corner into Geezerhood is that my last words will be "Linda...quick...pour me whatever little bit is left in that bottle of Calvados!"

Apropos of that change in my life (death, that is), the realization that this is that special occasion I've been saving all the good stuff for all these years, I am reminded of a recent dilemma of a good friend of mine who was found to have some incipient cardiac problems and was advised by his doctor that among a lot of other lifestyle changes he would have to stop drinking altogether. The problem for my friend is that he doesn't drink and hasn't for a couple decades now. I recommended that now he really didn't have much of a choice in the matter: since the doctor had laid down the law that he would have to stop drinking. What he would have to do is resume his former bad habits and take up drinking again. And then stop. Nothing is more important than 1) your health and 2) following your doctor's orders.

Along with shedding the jerks in your life, you will find a new appreciation for those you trust and love. And a new confidence in saying to them, "You are beautiful, I am so glad to have you for a friend, you are a blessing, and…I love you."

# CUTTING THE LIFELINE:

*[An author's note: A lot of men boast about their manly performance, if you know what I mean, and are drenched in embarrassment when they sense they are not up, as it were, to snuff, so to speak. I am neither of those kinds of man. Yes, in my bachelor days women referred to me as "Turbo," "Mr. Up And At 'Em," "The Energizer Bunny," and "Al-Night Roger." But enough of that. And I would be the first to admit occasional inadequacies. There was that time when I broke my foot and had a case of the fantods, for example. 1977, I think it was. But because of the delicate nature of the topic of this chapter—to wit,, winkie work—I have drawn more than ever on my creative spirit. None of the following is first-hand, in a manner of speaking. The stories here are composites of the tales of woe I have heard from other men, laments from classical literature, and in some cases my own inventions from my own fertile mind. The medical conditions are absolutely true, that is, but the cast of characters has been completely disguised. None of these stories about non-performance pertain to me. None. I've never had any sort of problem like this at all. I hadn't even <u>heard</u> of most of them until I talked with a doctor and did some reading. I am not*

*even sure how to spell "impotent." (Or is it "inpotent?" I wouldn't know.) Never had a problem with that. So if you have further questions, ask someone else, someone who has. Especially if you're a woman. Nope. Not me.]*

Probably the biggest change in the senior's lifestyle is going to be…uh…well…er…you know…in the sack. That's why the subject has come up already again and again in these pages. Heaven knows, our society winks, nods, nudges, giggles, and hints at the issue enough that the problem shouldn't come as a surprise and yet it always does. If not as a surprise, then as a disappointment. As they say, "The second thing that goes is your mind." So, for a moment, let's all agree to be uncomfortable and mature and talk about that number one issue of growing old: Geriatric Sex. (Okay, everyone over 40, all together now— "EEEEEEEUUUUUUWWWWW! GROSS!")

I was probably only 17 years old, over fifty years ago, when the man who was to become my first father-in-law recited a poem to me that I thought was vaguely funny, especially the first verse, but whose true message I was only later going to come to understand. I have no idea what the origins of this poem might be. All I can imagine is that it is based in the immutable truths of tradition. Its message is rich and important. Listen carefully, especially if you are young. Go ahead and laugh…but weigh the truth in these words:

Those olden days I oft remember,
Those youthful days of joy and fun,
When all my joints were lithe and limber.
Did I say all? Yes, all but one.

Now I'm getting daily older,
Those youthful days of joy have gone;
My joints are getting daily stiffer,
Did I say all? Yes, all but one.

When I was considering getting a vasectomy I talked the issue over with some friends, as men will do, and was led to believe by my old friend Russ that it was a procedure pretty much along the same lines as a haircut..."You can go in during lunch, get your 'delivery system' unhooked, and be back at your desk before the hour is over," he told me. Three days after my neutering I was still in bed in agony.

Maybe Russ is tougher than I am (but I doubt it) or maybe his doctor was more skilled. I don't know. I prefer to think along the lines I argue when Linda and I both get a cold or the flu and she gives me a bad time about being a big sissy. When she is sick, it amounts to a good hundred pounds less sick than when I am sick. I like to think that is difference between Linda and me, and I suspect it might also explain the difference in reactions to the procedure between Russ and me—in the case of my vasectomy the doctor was simply working with a much larger piece of machinery than Russ's, and thus the additional discomfort I felt. I'm pretty sure that is the deal.

And yet the most substantial consequence of my vasectomy was when I almost drowned because of it. I was with my buddy Eric (again) swimming along in the current in the river that runs at the edge of our farm here. A flood had washed out quantities of fence posts and telephone poles for miles upstream and he and I were floating the river with a length of rope, salvaging poles and posts from timber snags and sandbars along the way, tying them together, and steering the raft to my land where we could drag them from the water with a tractor and stack them up to be used later in repairing my own fences.

As Eric and I floated along in the now placid river on this beautiful, warm summer day, we had time to talk and I mentioned that I was thinking about a vasectomy but like any man I was having my doubts and questions about the operation. Eric casually remarked that he had gone through the most painful part of the procedure but had backed out at the very last minute. Hmmmm... "most painful part of the procedure..." Obviously I wanted more details.

He said that he had gone to the doctor's office at the appointed hour, was lying on the table with his equipment airing and ready for the requested adjustments. He said a nurse had shaved him...as they always do, even when it's not even remotely necessary, one might note yet once again in these pages...and had taped his Johnson Bar, as it is sometimes identified in polite company, up and out of the way for the doctor. The doctor came in and rolled up to the operating table a cart of knives, clamps, augers, wrenches, tree saws, ridge reamers, and other tools that simply swept Eric's courage away like a dandelion's fluff before a spring gale. And Eric said that at that point he had decided no thanks, he did not care to go through with the planned operation, so he excused himself with the doctor, got off the operating table, got dressed, and left, his landing gear still in its original condition.

"But...what about what you described as 'the most painful part of the procedure?' What was that about?" I asked, delivering precisely the softball straight line he had anticipated.

"Well," he said, "That was when the nurse took the tape off of my Johnson Bar and tore all the hair off my chest."

And I almost drowned.

I was 44 years old when I married Linda, 18 years my junior, so I was already used to hearing jokes about June and January marriages. I was well primed with the standard responses, the most popular of which is of course "If she dies, she dies." Whenever we showed up at the village tavern together and someone accused me of plying her with drink hoping I would "get lucky," my usual line was "Yeah, maybe she'll get a little tipsy and when we get home she'll go to sleep and leave me alone!" I boasted that Linda had scored a real bargain when she got me; for whatever my failings in bed might be, she couldn't deny that I saved her a lot of time.

But an interesting and substantial new element was added to the mix when medical science began to turn its attention to precisely this dimension of life by talking openly and dealing directly with male potency...or, as the case may be, impotency.

Curiously, the <u>idea</u> of such a pharmaceutical sexual aid was well within the folk imagination long before Viagra became a household word. It was my father who told me the story about the elderly gent who came into the tavern and uncharacteristically bought a round for everyone present, clearly feeling he had something to celebrate. When someone asked him the reason for his generosity, he said, "You know that bull I bought a few months back that turned out to be no good? I was talking with that new veterinarian just north of town and told him my problem and he said he had a new pill that just might solve the problem for me. He gave me a dozen of those pills but I had only given one to that bull when he showed new interest in the heifers, took care of all my cows, jumped the fence and dealt with the neighbor's cows too. The last I saw of him, that bull was headed down the road toward the dairy two miles away."

"Wow," said one of the fellows in the bar. "What do you suppose is in a pill like that that makes it so powerful?"

"I don't know," the old farmer said, "...but they taste like peppermint."

When I told my father that one, he immediately said said, "But that's not the end of that story. "Someone else said to the old guy, 'Did them pills do you any good then, old timer?' and he said, 'I should say so...I made love six times last night before midnight!'

"'And what did you wife have to say to that?'"

"'Don't know...haven't been home yet!'"

Again I laughed and again Dad said, "But that's not the end of the story. Someone asked the old timer, 'What did you do with the rest of them pills?' and he said, 'I threw 'em down the well...and haven't been able to get the pump handle down since!'"

And then to everyone's astonishment along came that little blue pill and what had been a joke became a reality. And it remained no less a joke, it seemed. Seniors boasted of taking Viagra...not to enhance their bedtime manner but to keep them from rolling out of bed. Out of nowhere at all, Linda told a visiting friend that the doctor had given us a year's supply of Viagra free. Six pills. My Dad used to brag that he and Mom well into their seventies "did it" almost every night of the week. They almost did in Monday, they almost did it on Tuesday, they almost did it on Wednesday….etc.

The gag lines seemed to write themselves sometimes, or at least the ad agencies delivered straight lines that couldn't be ignored. During an appointment with my doctor he asked if I had any questions and I said yes, that while it had nothing to do with my own situation (God knows!) I wondered about those warnings issued in television ads in regard to some potency enhancers that if a man taking the medication had an erection lasting over four hours, he should immediately contact a physician. I asked my doctor if he had ever encountered a case of a four-hour erection and what the heck he would do to alleviate that kind of problem. He said no, he had yet to encounter that side effect of the drug, but he supposed that the best way to deal the problem would be to send the sufferer over to the nurses' station.Or the patient call up one of his old girl-friends. Or suggest that his wife call her since she may be ready to pass the baton, so to speak, after the first hour or so. Maybe country doctors are just better at such things than those fancy city boys.

If you are innocent enough to still believe anything you see on television, where "reality" shows feature things that have absolutely nothing to do with reality, then you would think from the advertisements for "male enhancement" that half the men in this world have "e.d." (a polite way of saying "erectile dysfunction," which is a polite way of saying that when you have sex it's like shooting pool with a rope), while the other half are scientists working on a, er, wick stiffener, so to speak. And this of course leads to the other curious but obvious conclusion that women are all panting and pawing the ground just rarin' to jump in bed and do monkey tricks while at the same time being perfectly willing to wait until the Old Man figures out that he's just not going to get things done with Mr. Limp Biscuit, formerly known as Captain Happy. And of course there are the "natural" treatments of vitamin E, raw oysters, and ginseng tea, guaranteed by the Chinese to "restore your vitality," and we all know that the Chinese breed like rabbits. I mean, jeez, look at <u>China</u>! It's <u>full</u> of people. You'd think they were all Catholics! I made myself a big mug of ginseng tea this morning after giving Linda fair warning that she might want to schedule an extra long lunch hour and eat kind of light. Well, it's now 11:30 and I am not seeing a lot of signs, if you know what I mean, of increased, uh, vitality. So I went into the kitchen to give her a status report and she was making us braunschweiger and onion sandwiches for lunch. She says she just had a feeling about the whole plan.

I sense a disparity here in the television ads showing a man suddenly smiling, blinking sensitively at his wife, and her absolutely glowing at the news that, as the Cialas commercials phrase it, "the moment is right." For the gent maybe... A news program reported not long ago that a sexual torque amplifier (as the process is called for those of us who are tractor mechanics) had been developed for women. I rushed to the kitchen to tell Linda the good news. She said, "So...how do they get women to take it? Is it like we wrap the dogs' worming pills in a scrap of baloney and then toss it to them in the air so they've downed it before they know it? I can't imagine a woman taking a pill for 'enhancement,' unless maybe if they stick the pill in some really good chocolate and tossed it up into the air..."

I urge the pharmaceutical industry to cease and desist. This constant emphasis on wienie boosting is not healthy for America's ageing male population. As if it weren't bad enough that I have to sit in front of our television every night wondering what Linda is thinking when yet another advertisement for yet another "male enhancement formula" is aired, sometimes she makes it quite clear what she's thinking. Last night after a commercial for a magical wick stiffener named Enzyte, Linda said, "Male enhancement formula? What's it do...make him shave, take a shower, comb his hair, brush his teeth, and take you out for dinner and a movie?!" At times like this, it's good to practice a geezerly ploy called "Elective deafness."

But there is no help in appealing to a corporate conscience. Now the helpful people at Cialis are promoting a "36-hour e.d. medication" because "the moment might be right when you least expect it." At my age you can pretty much count on such an event being unexpected all right. Linda says a 36-hour mood elevator, so to speak, is designed to be "good for home, good for the office." Wives might want to check their husband's medications inventory. She says what is needed for most marriages is a 15-minute e.d. medication: take the pill, fall into the sack, wiggle, and exit. Save time, energy, and probably wear and tear on your PaceMaker. Use it and lose it, as Linda again notes

On the other hand, let's look at the silver lining to this, uh, diminished capability. A couple nights ago some called late in the evening and left a prank message on our answering machine in a late night call...a woman's voice: "Roger, Honey...just wanted to let you know not to come over tonight because my husband will be home. I'm sorry we can't have our special night. Let's make arrangements for another time...real soon, okay?" My first thought was how would this woman's husband being home have anything to do with me peeing just once that night, that being what the phrase "special night" means for me these days. For a brief moment Linda thought it might have something to do with a romantical tryst but she quickly dismissed that notion because 1) the voice was that of a young woman, 2) she obviously didn't know me because she called way too late to find me awake, and 3) Linda knows as well as I do that the term "special night" suggests all night, or at any rate more than the three-minute night (counting watching the evening news and maybe Leno's monologue) that have come to characterize our romantical interludeds. That would pretty much means the caller had the wrong Roger.

My years in a university anthropology department gave me some different perspectives on such things. For all our arrogance about the superiority of our own cultural system, any investigation at all suggests that we might have had a lot to learn from other societies from which we have apparently learned nothing. Our farm is on what was once Pawnee country and so I have a natural interest in that culture, one feature of which gives tired old gents like me something to chew on intellectually. Marriages in that tribe were more rationale and flexible than our own (where, however, if we were honest we'd admit that what we profess about the durability of our marital arrangements is a damnsite more strict than the reality; if you doubt me, look in Wikipedia under Larry King, Elizabeth Taylor, or Tiger Woods). I find it hilarious that some small-minded people consider same sex unions to be a threat to marriage when it seems pretty clear to me that the biggest threat to marriage is mixed gender marriages. Nothing causes divorce, as my father used to say, like marriage. But a part of Pawnee life that certainly gives us geezers something to mull over on quiet winter evenings is that sexual liaisons were usually made between older gents and younger women. And between older women and younger men.

It's not at all a bad idea, if you think about it. (And I do.) Old men aren't going to make a lot of demands, aren't in all that much of a hurry, have some idea what they are doing, and are inclined in such situations to be grateful. Enormously grateful. A young woman who was bedding with an elderly friend of mine once told me when I wondered what the heck a lovely, lithe creature like her was gracing the life of this old geezer friend of mine, she said sweetly, "I like doing it with old guys. They are always so grateful."

And the same is true of older women…patient and knowledgeable, and perfectly acceptable to the young man who really doesn't care what he couples with as long as it's warm and soft. Or at least warm. Or at least soft. Or not. See? Everyone in a Pawnee village wound up happy. Damn savages.

Nor is the cultural zest of Pawnee culture dead within the tribe. A Pawnee tribal elder was visiting us here at our farm not long ago, and as if to issue a gentle compliment to Linda said, "You know, in our culture it is the tradition that the host offers a visitor the bedroom company of his wife during the visit." I said that in all my reading of Pawnee culture, I hadn't run across that custom before. Linda said she thought she'd read it somewhere. Young women…old men. Yeah, I guess that works all right.

If there is one problem with this theory it's that young women have a certain, uh, well… <u>frankness</u> that can be occasionally disconcerting. Read that story above about the visiting Pawnee elder again. That's the kind of thing I'm thinking about. A woman I was working with a few years ago was sound asleep one night when her husband came in late and started to get into bed with her when out of her dead sleep she called him… Roger. He did not find that slip of the lip at all amusing (they are now divorced) but I found it wonderfully flattering and amusing, as did this woman. And so did her compatriots at work when she made the mistake of blabbing the story around the table at the first coffee break. When the word got back to me I instantly broadcast the tale even further…being trained as a folklorist, after all…only slightly enhancing the narrative to the effect that when her husband crawled between the sheets, she screamed out my name in orgiastic ecstasy. (It is widely and generally acknowledged in talltale circles that each teller is entitled to improve any story by ten percent at each telling and while I may have exceeded that a bit…maybe by a factor of a thousand…in this case it seemed worth whatever penalty the authorities regulating competitive mendacity might impose on me.)

And then I went straight to the house and repeated the story to Linda, adding, "Well, my dear, I'd say that you have something of a bit of competition when it comes to Kay!" And without so much as looking up from her newspaper, Linda said, "Tell her she can have you Tuesdays, Thursdays, and every other weekend."

I could tell she was being eaten alive by jealousy.

Painfully similar was her response last year when she asked me what I wanted for my birthday and I joked that maybe this would be the appropriate occasion for that threesome I'd always wanted. To my amazement…you'd think that sooner or later I'd get over be amazed by Linda's way of thinking but to this day I am never even close to anticipating that two-by-four blow between my eyes…to my amazement, she said, "Fine. It's okay with me if you have a threesome party in bed. Go right ahead and help yourself. But I do want you to understand I won't be one of the women at the party."

Huh? My wife is giving me approval for sexual debauchery with two women…and furthermore is opting out and thus suggesting I take not just one but two women to the pinnacles of delight with me?! I don't think I said a word at that point. I am sure I couldn't even think of a word at that point. But bright and sensitive woman that Linda is, she sensed my confusion and explained, "Look, Rog…the chances of you finding another woman who will get into bed naked with you is…what?…maybe one in a million? So…what do you think are the odds against you finding two women who would get into bed naked with you? At the same time…?! Can't even be calculated…. They don't make numbers that big."

One of Linda's favorite jokes is the one about the guy who dies and himself being led down a long, brilliant white hallway lined with doors. Finally his white robed escort stops at a door opens it and directs the man in, where he sees Cindy Crawford lying naked on a huge, round, slowly turning bed, satin sheets, candles, soft music. The man asks the escort, "Is it true? Have I died and gone to heaven?" and the escort explains, "No, Cindy Crawford died…and has gone to hell."

# ACCIDENT PRONE, PRONE ACCIDENTS, ETC.

Let's just say for the sake of conversation that your health is fine. The doctor says you are in excellent condition for your age. You eat healthy, exercise regularly, think clean thoughts, wear sensible shoes... So, you're safe, right? Wrong-o! It's out there waiting for you, and the longer it waits, the surer you can be that it's gonna get you. It's like those people you see running along highways for their health, sucking in the automobile exhaust fumes, apparently unaware that all kinds of people with considerably less concern about their health are coming up behind them at excessive speed, talking on a cell phone, texting (for gods' sake! What kind of idiot types a letter while driving at 80 miles an hour on a four-lane speedway?), eating their sixteenth breakfast burrito, talking with someone in the backseat (all the while maintaining eye contact of course, driving a car that is serviceable only because the geniuses in your state legislature were bought off by the used car lobby and retracted the laws about safety inspections). And they are aiming right at the reflective stripes on the back of your tee shirt.

You think I'm joking, right? Well, just let ol' Rog tell you a true story. I was recovering nicely from my first cardiac event, losing weight and working at getting into shape by walking up into town a mile each way every day to get the mail. Safety? You bet! I'm no idiot! I was walking on a village street, not along the highway after all. And I was on the left side of the wide road. I was alert to my surroundings, noting a huge green tractor coming out of the Co-op with a large feed bunker in its loader, pulling a big trailer loaded with a bale-buster and sacks of feed supplement. But hey, he was either going to turn left and away from me, or right and be way over on the other side of the road. There was no other traffic...never is in a little town like mine, nothing obscuring me walking along, and the tractor driver was high up in a wide open cab with visibility as if he'd been sitting atop of thirty-foot pole in the middle of an open Plains pasture. So without giving the big Deere a second thought, I marched on down the road, my mail bag draped jauntily over my shoulder.

And the next thing I knew I had been thrown violently to the ground by a ferocious blow from behind, right on that selfsame mail bag, and I was lying in the gravel of the road looking up at the undercarriage of a gigantic John Deere tractor passing over me, its enormous tires rolling on either side of my pathetically vulnerable body.

After the ambulance got there and gathered me up out of the ditch where I had rolled, the driver explained that part of his load had dropped off the trailer and he looked back to see what he had lost. Suddenly, All he knew was that he was on the wrong side of the road and I was lying in the gravel under him dodging those gigantic tires. I couldn't blame the tractor driver—I've made the same mistake myself, even with a tractor. But this time I was the one on the ground, and I was hurt.

Since the accident happened in town, the EMTs were there almost instantly, needing to come only a couple town blocks to reach the scene of the accident. As they cleaned the dirt and gravel from my superficial head wounds, I waved them off, explaining that that was not a result of the tractor accident but was probably the consequences from when I walked home late from the tavern the night before. They figured if I was still up to laughing, I probably hadn't been mortally wounded.

I managed to pull myself together and get back home without going to the hospital but in a couple days it was clear that all was not well inside this battered old body and I needed someone to take a look. The doctor's verdict was that I had a couple broken or cracked ribs...not much to be done there...and a broken left hand. (The surprise there was that the x-ray showed that my left hand had been broken before but never properly set. Some stray bones were drifting around or were stuck in unlikely positions, but I had no recollection at all about when that might have happened. I guess that says something about my lifestyle, huh?)

I recovered from those injuries, but as I would soon learn was going to be the new standard of my developing Geezerhood, the wounds would never completely be forgotten like the first time I had broken that left hand. Now my every injury lingers on and comes back to remind me of the event whenever it is cold or when I put pressure on it in just a slightly wrong way or sometimes for no apparent reason at all.

And the lesson I had learned long ago from my father and had re-enforced at every step...or rather, misstep...of my life comes back to me with some regularity: you can piss and moan or you can giggle and laugh. Life is a funny thing because it can be a tragedy or a comedy, depending in large part pretty much on how you look at it. Kinda like sex. Nothing is funnier than sex, if you look at it with any sort of objectivity. And yet nothing is more serious. There's actually no reason why it can't be both. Same with life.

The next day after I was run down by the big John Deere tractor (and one needs to understand the irony of this...I have some notoriety as an Allis Chalmers man when it comes to tractors, a lover of the orange and demeanor of the greener, so there was something of a richness of irony in the fact that I had been smacked down and run over by a big Deere!) there was a homemade sign mounted on a post at the site of the accident reading CAUTION! UNMARKED DEERE CROSSING and a neighbor met me at the Post Office to hand me an orange caution vest with a big SLOW MOVING VEHICLE triangle sewn onto the back. "Friends" commented publicly that the accident was my own darn fault...I wasn't wearing a WIDE LOAD sign, after all...and the most common question among the gossips was whether Linda, a John Deere enthusiast—we're a mixed marriage-- was the driver of the offending assault tractor. Eric said that he heard it was the same old problem rearing its ugly head yet again...me chasing vehicles through town, barking and biting at tires.

Up until I was maybe 60 I could say...if it wasn't true, I didn't know about it...that I had never broken a bone. Then one Christmas Eve I was working at picking up a big, heavy elm log for a Yule log because my son and his wife were going to arrive in a matter of minutes to celebrate the holidays with us. I found the huge hunk of heavy wood that struck my fancy and was working it off the top of the be-snowed, frozen woodpile when it unexpectedly broke loose and fell...right on top of my right foot. My foot instantly swelled up to the size of the log I was trying to move and as soon as we could get my boot and sock off, it was clear that we needed to get me to the emergency ward. Yep, X-rays showed that my foot was indeed broken. Enroute, about four miles from our home, we saw my son and his wife arriving from Minneapolis. We waved cheerily and figured we could explain the situation when we got back home from the emergency ward. That was when I first started to aquire the Geezer Gait, and kind of bent over to one side hobble, with maybe a shuffle and a hitch in the get-along.

There's no sense in going into an inventory of all the injuries I have suffered in my shop where I rebuild old tractors because there it has only been an intensification of a long, long history: I have always hurt myself in my shop. Or outside my shop. The only change in my regularly scheduled accidents has been that as I have gotten older, the injuries come along more frequently and with more dire consequences. And the damage heals more slowly with every new affliction. About all we can hope for once we get to our hahahahahaha Golden Years is that when you get a knee injury, it will be on the leg opposite of the one you injured last time so you can balance out the limp.

I was actually being pretty careful when I spent a day mowing around the farmstead to knock down enough grass and brush to slow down any winter prairie fires started along the highway by some careless idiot discarding a cigarette. I avoided the whirling blades of the shredder (on that occasion at least; once before I'd leaned into the shredder blade and wound up with a badly bruised knee), and the incredibly dangerous shaft of the power take-off power the mower from the tractor drive train. I was seated securely, and I went neither too fast nor too slow for conditions. So…out of nowhere one of the front axles broke, digging the front of the tractor into the soft sand and pitching me forward in the tractor seat and into the vertical post of the front end loader. (For the information of those of you who are city slickers, one never wears a seat belt on a tractor without a roll bar, always wears one where there is a roll bar. This tractor had no roll bar and thus no seat belt.) To this day two years later I am still having trouble with that blasted knee; the doctor says sooner or later we'll have to replace it with a mechanical equivalent but I say not yet…I'm still waaaaay too young! I almost think I should ease off on the medication and encourage the gout in the other knee which would balance out the limp and I would march along with an even gait.

Of all the things I've recognized by way of change over my long and lovely life, one of the worst is what the Republicans have done to gravity. That's why I snort when anyone refers to right-wingers as "conservatives." No one is more determined to change the nature of mankind, life, love, and nature than the so-called "conservatives," and the worst of the disasters those benighted souls have visited on us is their plot to ratchet gravity up from (I would guess…I'm not a physicist) about 50% on the gravity gauge to something closer to 87.3 %. It seems like I can't hold anything in my hands any more with it hitting the floor somewhere along the line. I can set down just about anything from a rock to book on something as flat as a table and sure as can be, it's going to fall on the ground or the floor within minutes, if not seconds. I spend half my time bending over and picking things up.

And the other half of the time picking myself up off the ground or the floor. Sure, the increase in gravity makes the fall faster and easier but then the problem is that it makes it twice as hard for me to get vertical again.

It is a med school lesson…there are entire semester classes devoted to this…for doctors to insist that you lose weight. If they have nothing else to say, it'll be "It would be a good idea for you to lose some weight, Rog." Dentists tell you to floss. It's a dental rule. No one does of course but then they comfortably charge you double time because they have given you good advice. Ask any lawyer if anything will be a good idea and they will always say, "No." That way they are safe. And they can charge you double. Doctors tell you to lose weight. You have bad feet? "Lose weight." Male pattern baldness" "Lose weight." Can't pay your bills? "Lose weight." Save yourself $200 and skip your next trip to a doctor's office; just go up to the town tavern and have a buddy up there tell you to lose weight. Which you could probably do by not going up to the tavern. Which reminds me of the old joke about the geezer whose doctor tells him his hearing trouble is a result of over-drinking and so the only way he is going to get his hearing back is to lay off the suds. To which the old timer mumbles, "I like what I'm drinkin' more than what I'm hearin'."

Well, I'm telling you to pay no attention to that nonsense. Okay, maybe if you'd lose weight you wouldn't fall down quite as often, or even as hard, but without that padding you're also going to hit the floor or the ground a lot harder. Think of it as…padding. I have taken to carrying an Alpine hiking staff because you will also find that less and less you fall down close to something to help yourself back up. But I am way too young to use a cane, so I carry an Alpine hiking staff. Or Wanderstock.

See? That makes me sound almost like a mountain climber instead of a hobbling old geezer.

Worst of all, the Republican increase in gravity has also directly affected my old body. I can see gravity's effect everywhere. Where muscles used to ripple, there are now slow flesh and flab slides. And what has sunken ever lower seems ever more difficult to bring back up, if you catch my drift.

Another thing you can be rock-certain sure of, whenever you have accidents…fall, drop something, have a heart attack, stroke, bad burn, huge cut, a crippling bout of gout…it will be sometime between a late Friday afternoon and dawn Monday. It never fails It proves there's a god.

Speaking of gout, did you know that misery is not the rich man's affliction it was once thought to be? It isn't Yorkshire pudding, fine port, and Stilton cheese that cause spikey little acid crystals the size of a pin head but with the impact of a basketball to form in your knee cap or toe joints. No, it's peasant things like beer and beans--that is to say, my kind of food. The only good thing about gout is that one way of alleviating the horrible pain is cherries. And I like cherries. I once remarked to a doctor and his nurse that while I had never experienced childbirth myself, I have seen childbirth a couple times and it is clearly my impression that the pain of gout is worse. I expected the nurse to throttle me on the spot, aided by Linda, but no, the nurse said after a thoughtful pause, "You know, Rog, I have gone through both childbirth and gout and you are right: gout is worse." There is an upside to gout and believe me, any good you can dredge out of this curse is worth considering. A traditional and effective preventative against gout is…cherries. You know, like cherry pie, cherry tarts, chocolate-covered cherries, cherry herring liqueur, cherry cider…. You know what they say you should do when life gives you lemons. Well, that goes double for gout. When life gives you gout, eat cherry pie.

In the spirit of the bikers who bunch up and ride in parades and around the rural countryside roaring, looking tough, and "supporting the troops," or gaggles of sorority girls who play marathon tennis games to raise funds to buy textbooks for Eskimo children, or rich businessmen who meet for drinks and lunch, exchange jokes, and con someone into giving a free program because they are "a non-profit 'service' organization," I have resolved to dedicate myself to establishing and funding a foundation to find a definitive cure for...gout! And I am going to reveal that grand plan to banish forever the misery of gout right here and now, in these pages—to wit, viz: The Roger Welsch Anti-Gout Pie-a-Thon!

Here are the details, so you can start your participation in this noble effort right now:

1.  Those of you who care about the suffering of your fellow man, send me a pie. Of course cherry pie would be splendidly appropriate but in the spirit of diversity, feel free to substitute (in this order):

    Pecan pie
    Lemon meringue
    Chocolate
    Cocoanut cream
    Key lime
    Strawberry (strawberry-rhubarb acceptable)
    Apple
    Peach
    Chocolate cake or carrot cake with cream cheese frosting at least a half-inch thick would also work.
    Or brownies
    Or Pineapple upside down cake
    Or a couple of the really big Snickers bars like they sell at truck stops

2.  Then for each pie I eat, I will pester and extort someone, probably the same belabored businesses that sponsor (that is, pay good money) for the dumb stuff bikers, service clubs, and sorority girls do, to send me, oh, ten, or twenty, or even a hundred dollars per eaten pie to find that cure

for gout. Like buying more cherry pie. See? It's a little like Pies-for-Pesos! (Note also page 173, "Geezer Make-a-Wish Foundation")

Now, where was I? Oh yeah…vehicular accidents…. What I do worry about is not driving a tractor, even on the rough ground of our river uplands, but driving an automobile. It's not so much that I worry about myself as I am concerned about what my creeping incompetence behind the wheel might mean by way of jeopardy for others. Moreover, it's not so much my stiff knee or broken hand…that is the clearly physical…that makes me uneasy about driving but the diminution of my senses and reactions…eyesight and hearing in particular. I'm no slouch when it comes to driving: I haven't had an accident in fifty years now and I am a graduate of the Bondurant School of High Performance Driving, both the stock car and the grand prix open-wheel race car stages. But can you guess what it is that scares me and makes me especially cautious about my driving and how my ageing might affect it?

It's something I learned at the Bondurant driving school. The most common tool in America is the automobile. There are probably more people in America with automobiles than claw hammers. And yet there probably is no tool with which Americans are less well trained, experienced, or thoughtful with than the automobile. Do you doubt that assertion? Drive fifteen minutes and watch the idiots around you. There's your proof. Does it look like these half-wits have any notion of the damage they can do with that huge machine and the completely incompetent, dangerous way they are handling…or not handling…it?

The two worst classes of drivers on our roads today are 1) irresponsible kids driving like they are never going to die and 2) irresponsible elders driving as if they don't care if they die. There is no more excuse for someone over 80 years of age to be driving than there is for anyone under 18 to be driving. That assertion isn't going to make me any friends among my contemporaries, I know, but it's true. Go to any senior center or retirement home and watch some frail, little, blue-haired lady stagger along, barely mobile even with a walker to lean on, unsteady, uncertain, too weak to open a door for herself, unable to hear or understand your offer of assistance, squinting at you through glasses that haven't been upgraded since shortly after the Korean War...and then share my dismay as this same totally irresponsible person pulls herself laboriously, dragging her oxygen bottle cart behind her...into a car the size and weight of an armored personnel carrier and then, peering intently through the steering wheel, utterly unable to see anything within twenty feet of the bumper of the war wagon she is trying to operate, launches herself into the urban traffic battleground. Or worse yet, heads out onto the highway where she can create even greater chaos and mayhem at high speed. What kind of madness is that? You don't believe me? I dare you—go sit in the parking lot or lobby of any senior citizen home or center for an hour and there's not a doubt in my mind that you will see at least one totally incapacitated person struggling out the door with a walker or wheel chair...and into a high-powered automobile to ricochet his or her way through the neighborhoods between the nursing home parking lot and her target for the day. They all say the same thing: "I'll know when it's time for me to stop driving."

Just three days ago at this writing, an elderly woman at the retirement home where my mother lived had a bit of a driving mishap. My mother, 91 years of age at the time and whom I not too gently argued into surrendering her license and her car a couple years ago, has expressed envy for this woman. She is well into her 80's, but dang it, she has her car, a BattleBoat Buick with an extra high steering wheel periscope she peers through to see over the hood of the gunboat. She drives when and wherever she wants to. Even to the nearby city on a high-speed four-lane highway, where she maneuvers uncertainly through congested traffic...as I said, any time, anywhere she wants. Now, that is real freedom—endangering lives every second she is behind that wheel. Who insures these people? Who issues them driving licenses? Where are their families?

Saturday she apparently wanted to drive through the crossbars and lights into the side of a speeding train, because that's what she did. No one can figure out what might have gone wrong. Of course she was stone deaf so she couldn't hear the train, yet the warning bells. And she can't see much, so that might have been the problem. She can barely get around with her walker so I imagine it might have been that she couldn't get her foot off of the accelerator, or maybe onto the brake pedal, or maybe press at all hard enough to slow down, yet stop, since she can't so much as negotiate a two-inch step. Or maybe it was her reaction time, which is down to something like an hour and a half by now. Yep, it's a real mystery. It's just a shame she didn't have her problem when she was approaching a school crosswalk loaded with children. That way there wouldn't have been nearly as much damage to her car.

Last time Mom talked with this inadvertent street terrorist about driving, she spoke the ultimate Geezerly idiocy: "Oh, I'll know when it's time for me to stop driving." I'm guessing it was about a tenth of a second after she hit the side of that speeding train, if not a trifle before. Folks, please, if you are over the age of 70, for God's sake, just give it up. Show some of the maturity and good sense you should have accumulated by now. Take a cab. Stay at home. Ask someone else to give you a ride. But get the hell out from behind that wheel before you kill someone other than yourself, someone who doesn't deserve it nearly as much as you do.

If this kind of geriatric lunacy is a disgrace when women do it, it is even worse with men because way too many men consider an automobile an extension of their manhood. Since the real thing has sort of abandoned them, they therefore feel all the more ferocious about the kind they can start with a key. I recall with considerable pain the first time I suggested to Dad it might be time to turn over the wheel to Mom or maybe even just get rid of the car and use alternative forms of transportation. I might just as well have suggested that he cheer for Kansas State against Nebraska in a football game. Never mind that his various incapacities contributed to an accident in the city and an almost fatal one on the Interstate. He used the standard inanity of the overaged driver, "I'll know when it's time for me to stop driving." The honest, frank, and sad fact of the matter is that people like this never do know when it's time for them to stop driving.

I have an uncle still on the streets in an automobile who has to phone home frequently to get directions where he is going even though he goes the same place and only that same place once a week. If he gets more than one city block off his customary path, someone has to go retrieve him. He has no idea where he is or where he is going. Why doesn't someone worry enough about him enough to cut the fuel line on that car? Why doesn't someone care enough about children on their way to school or people crossing the crosswalk with a bag of groceries to simply say "What car?" the next time he goes out and finds the garage empty? Why doesn't our society use common sense and see to it that the elderly can get where they want and need to go without endangering themselves and everyone around them every time they drag themselves behind the steering wheel of two tons of steel? How proud is this fine old man going to be when he sits on the witness stand and explains how it came to be that utterly incapable of even the simplest processes of life he has now killed three children when he was trying to negotiate city traffic in a vehicle he wasn't even vaguely in physical control of?

What about me? How is my driving, you ask? Well...uh... I'll know when it's time for me to stop driving! Hahahahahahaha! But seriously, folks, I rarely drive any more, far preferring to sit back and relax while much younger Linda handles the wheel. I don't want to be that sorry old geezer on the witness stand either.

I imagine it's easier to make this mistake in judging one's own driving competence in a small town like the one here where I live. There's one little old lady here who of course muscles around our village streets a gigantic Belchfart Hellfire about half as long as a football field. Everyone knows her and her car and makes a frantic maneuver to get off the street any time they see her headed in their direction. Someone should mount a flashing yellow light on top of her car because she is an accident just looking for a venue. There was the time when she entered the drive-through entrance of Maxine's beauty shop, for example. No, there hadn't been a drive-through entry there previously and yes, Maxine and her customers were somewhat surprised when the old lady's gunboat came through the front wall, but then they saw who was driving and they weren't surprised at all.

You think I'm kidding? Well, the local mechanics finally got tired of installing new starting motors in this selfsame woman's car. Being stone deaf (along with being blind and crippled) she could never tell when her car started and was running, so she just kept turning the key and grinding away at the Bendix until the starting motor burned out. About once a week or so, in fact. Now, wouldn't you think it was about time someone this disabled got out from behind the Death Machine and retired her IMSA racing license? But no, the solution for her was to have the town mechanic take a sledge and knock the muffler off her car's exhaust system. Now she can hear when her engine is running. And so can everyone else within six miles of town, which is actually a very good thing because it gives a wider margin for everyone to get his vehicle tucked away somewhere safe when she fires up her Sherman tank and takes to the streets.

It's really pretty funny... you hear the roar of that monster engine and instantly people come tumbling out the café, tavern, bank, and grocery store to save their vehicles. Thing is, she can't see behind her—she's not tall enough to look over the back of the driver's seat or get any kind of scope from the rearview mirror—so she just revs the engine, pops the clutch, and lurches back until she hits something. Then she drops it into drive and goes forward. Hopefully her carom cushion is a light pole or maybe a concrete curb and not your new pickup truck, but if it is...you can hardly complain. You were warned.

# COMMON AND OTHER SENSES:

The venerable joke about the three old ladies on the bus is again making the rounds. I think the first time I heard it was, no kidding, when I was in junior high school.

FIRST OLD LADY: It certainly is windy today.

SECOND OLD LADY: No, you're wrong. I think it's Thursday.

THIRD OLD LADY: Me too! How about stopping in to the tavern for a cold one?

Nothing more clever than making fun of some geezer's diminished capacities. At least not until you are the geezer in question. Or Geezerette. For me deafness seemed to happen all at once. One day I was fine, and the next I had an incessant, overwhelming ringing in my ears, which I have now enjoyed for twelve years. We went to hearing specialists, we tried hearing aids...nothing works. The up-side is that after all these years I understand my parents' hearing problems...and have come to appreciate not only the problems of not hearing what's going on but also the comfort that can come from that. Especially about the time of the evening news every day. Or political campaigns every four years. My father had his timing nailed down: I would approach him as he relaxed in his chair reading the newspaper and say, "Pop, I was wondering if maybe…" and with one deft sweep of his hand he would flick the volume control on his hearing aid and calmly go back to reading his paper. Believe me, there are some things you want to hear…and more than you might expect that you don't. Besides, at my age I've heard almost everything already and I really don't need to hear much of it again.

Linda is an excellent communicator. She says more things with fewer words than anyone I know. We were once watching a news bulletin about a woman who had poisoned her husband with a tea made from the common houseplant oleander because he had turned off his hearing aid and refused to listen to whatever she had to say. I was still sitting there stunned by this horrendous crime when Linda said quietly, "Rog…Rog…would you like a cup of tea?" I heard that quite clearly, even without a hearing aid.

Another time I was eating supper, noting that Linda had done a particularly nice job with the meat entrée. She had stepped into the kitchen, so I called to her, "Hon, what did you marinate this meat in?" She came out all gooey eyed and hugged me, saying, "Of course! That is one of the nice things you've ever said to me." I was understandably bewildered and said, "Uh, what do you think I just said?"

"Didn't you ask me if I would marry you again?"

"No," I laughed, "I said, 'What did you marinate this meat in?!'" And she went back into the kitchen. And having thought about the confusion, I yelled again, "Hey Hon…<u>would</u> you marry me again?"

Without coming out of the kitchen she yelled back, "Vinegar and soy sauce!"

As we later agreed, no matter what Dr. Phil says, the real secret to a successful relationship is communication. Even for Geezers.

Often the difficulties of ageing are not so much a matter of us changing as they are of the world changing around us. For example, I increasingly find that none of my clothes fit, obviously a matter of the world going metric while I remain well-grounded in good old American inches and feet. Same with my eyes. Obviously printers are using smaller and smaller typefaces, making it increasingly hard to read printed material. I know my eyes are still good because I still spot things that much younger eyes do not. All I need to do is spend a few minutes in the city, for example, and I see boys and girls with their pants falling down which I can see just plain as a plumber's cleavage, something you would think they would notice themselves. But they don't.

Other than my eyeglasses becoming ever harder to find mornings, I find that the biggest problem is that they seem to require constant adjustment. We are forever in the eyewear department of the store where we get our glasses, getting them readjusted and tightened. It seems that as we get older, after 25 years of marriage, my glasses show special stress and wear from me moving my head up and down in a nodding motion while, curiously, Linda's glasses require constant reworking from the strain of being shaken repeatedly from side to side.

As we approach our dotage the computer in our head does curious things with our memories too…kind of like one of those computer viruses or worms they talk about. Now, I want to make it clear that memory has never been one of my strongest assets as it is. Linda insists to this day that she has marked prominently on her calendar the remarkable day when I both 1) threw something away and 2) remembered where I put my billfold. I operate on the system described so well by my buddy Lunchbox: Each morning I make a list of what I have to do that day and then I know I am done when I lose the list.

A dear old friend of mine once told me that one of the reason he hated cats was that they are so stupid, they frequently wander into a room and then stand there puzzled because quite clearly they have forgotten why they came in there in the first place. He said that was the reason he hated cats…at least until more and more he started doing the same thing. Conversations between Linda and me have become so disconnected, we have developed a code phrase for what happens when we are moving along in one conversational direction when all of a sudden things somehow switch to a completely different topic. Somewhere Linda got a T-shirt that says "SOME PEOPLE SAY I HAVE ATTENTION DEFICIT SYNDROME BUT I DON'T THINK I DO BECAUSE...OH!...LOOK! *A CHICKEN!*" All we have to do therefore to explain conversational confusion resulting from an unexplained and unexpected direction change is to say while looking elsewhere, "Oh!...Look!...A chicken!!!"

I have the feeling everyone has to deal with the mystery of what happens to odd socks in the laundry but I am not convinced that everyone has the same problem I do with things like socket wrenches, overalls, hotel keys, stocking caps and gloves, pry bars, pajamas, maps and magazines, television remote controls, flashlights, watches, and children. I have a very hard time imagining that it is all my fault that such things go astray so often. Isn't there a piece of literature somewhere about a wife or maybe children who drive a man to eventual madness by hiding things from him? I know I read that somewhere but now I can't remember where I put the book.

One of the most common expressions of my Geezerhood is "Wait a minute...did I already tell you this?" At least I am in the early stages of what they call "old-timers disease" around here. Eventually, I imagine, I will be like so many geezers and simply tell the same story over and over, one telling barely ending before the next begins, never even stopping to ask the question "Did I already tell you this?" But in a way that would be better than my current stage where I'm never sure. I now have the almost constant nagging feeling that I told this story about I'm about to launch into...oh, maybe an hour ago. And was it to this person or another? As a result, I probably wind up telling the same story over and over but without the forgiving grace of not remembering that I've already told it. Does that make any sense at all? Or...did I already tell you all that earlier in these pages?

I probably should print up another card like the Harmless Old Geezer hand-out that says something like "Please excuse the bearer if he already told you this story last week. Or yesterday. Or a quarter hour ago. Please humor him and pretend to listen attentively while he rattles on. Perhaps you can make a mental list of what you need at the grocery store or something like that or do a Soduko or crossword puzzle so the time isn't wasted."

In fact, I probably should print up another card like the Harmless Old Geezer hand-out that says something like "Please excuse the bearer if he already told you this story last week. Or yesterday. Or a quarter hour ago. Please humor him and pretend to listen attentively while he rattles on. Perhaps you can …." Wait a minute. Have I already told you this…?

Earlier today my sister-in-law asked me about something about Linda's plans and I had to reply that I really had no idea what she was up to because "These days nobody tells me anything." Then I had to admit the reality of the situation… "Or else they tell me…and I forget. It's one of those things."

On the other hand…there are always two sides to the story… Geezerhood's tendency toward a failing memory also has the advantage that even while you are forgetting you told this same audience this very same story only a half hour ago, you are also forgetting the story that they told you! This makes family reunions, drinking sessions with your buddies, and visits to the Old Veterans Home much easier on the constitution.

YOU: …And so that's the story about how I got this scar on my fanny. Pretty funny, huh?

ELDERLY FRIEND: That really is a good one…and I can see how my story about when I was in the break-out from the Pusan Reservoir during the Korean Conflict made you think of it.

YOU: It's curious, isn't it, how our lives are so far apart and yet when you boil them down, we're all pretty much alike in this world, huh?

ELDERLY FRIEND: You got that right, buddy. In fact, for some reason I was just thinking about the time I was in the army and the damned Commies had us cornered at the Pusan Reservoir. It was cold as hell, you know, and…

YOU: Excuse me for interrupting...I am really excited about hearing history from someone who was actually there...but after you tell me all about your experiences at Pusan, remind me to tell you...speaking of cold...about how I got this scar on my fanny.

ELDERLY FRIEND: Roger Wilco! Okay, see, there we were with nothing but the damn Chinks all around us...

See? Everyone is happy with the historical narrative tape cassette looping 'round and 'round and 'round...

In the hahahahahahaha Golden Years all this is intensified. As you age, just as you get more and more physical afflictions that last longer and therefore come to overlap so you are never without something or another wrong, you will find that you gradually but inevitably start losing more and more things for longer and longer periods, so you no longer lose your favorite pen...and then find it...and then lose the checkbook, but you lose the pen, and then the checkbook, and then the car keys and then your wife, which, if you think about it, can be approached as something of an economy because you can now look for six things at once instead of just one. And when you go to the doctor's office, it's no longer for some silly little thing you shouldn't even bother about, it's six or eight silly little things...making the trip worthwhile. Sometimes it seems like everything is falling apart all at once: a friend of mine has his telephone answering machine programmed to respond to incoming calls with the message, "This is Tom...or at least what's left of him."

Linda isn't nearly as old as I am but then she has a lot more details to keep track of too...for example, all the things I've done wrong over the last 26 years. She maintains that if she were just a little smarter, she'd be an idiot savant. As a friend of mine says...also a geezer...when he has yet another brain fart, as they have come to be called, "That's what I get for trying to use my brain twice in one day."

As if you haven't already figured it out, I am a storyteller. Always have been. Which doesn't mean that you simply report events as you see them, or invent things out of whole cloth. The trick of storytelling is to find the nugget of narrative in an anecdote and then, uh... improve it. Let's face it, God is not a very good storyteller. The timing of his reality is bad—too fast in some places, too slow in others, the characters are poorly developed and erratically motivated, the plot is poorly organized, each life seems to be more a matter of random coincidence than deliberate good sense. The task of the storyteller is simply to put things right again, to improve on God's sloppy composition skills.

One of the most unexpected changes in my physiology as I passed through the gates of time into my hahahahaha Golden Years (yeah, I know it sounds romantic but before you go too far down that path think again about all those ads you see every night on television of hemorrhoids, impotence, constipation, or adult diaperage) were the changes in my foodways. Hell, when I was younger, I could eat anything, and I pretty much did. I take enormous pride in the fact that there is only one thing in my entire life of looking at what's on the plate that I couldn't eat. I won't disgust you by telling you what that was. But other than that, I ate everything...including among many other items, dog, whale, squirrel, shark, squid, raccoon, alligator, kangaroo, eel, rattlesnake, buffalo intestine (boiled but also raw with a drop of fresh bison bile), corn smut, beaver tail, conch serviche, walrus, seal, snails, ostrich, snapping turtle, goat, and lemon chicken. But now I find that sure, I can still eat a nice big chunk sirloin smothered in onions and mushrooms...but if I eat it after five pm I might just as well plan on staying up to watch old movies well into the night because I sure won't be getting much sleep.

What's even worse, I used to be able to eat not just anything, but any amount of anything and, while I never in my life could have been described as "sylph-like," whatever I ate was translated fairly efficiently and fairly quickly into energy. Now I have no energy no matter what I eat or how much I eat, and I gain massive amounts of weight, no matter how carefully I eat or how little I eat.

I have my theories about this and none of them has much to do with what I eat or how much. That is to say, I am taking a governmental approach to this and insisting that I am not responsible. In the case of my weight however, it isn't all the fault of right-wing nuts and their conspiracy to increase gravity but rather of some skinny girl in New York City. I think it's all explained somewhere in Newton's Third Law of Caloric Dynamics: there are only so many adipose pounds in the universe and so no pounds are ever actually gained or lost in the world but are simply shuffled around from one frame to another. Thus, when the skinny girl in New York, aspiring to be a handbag model throws up her lunch of watercress salad, she loses a pound...and someone somewhere, about half the time some poor schmuck named Roger in Nebraska, gains that same pound even if he had nothing for supper but a can of sardines and saltines. So my impression is quite right: it doesn't matter what I do at the supper table, I am going to gain weight. That's all there is to it. I'm going to gain weight.

There are things the Geezer can do about this problem. You do have choices. For example, you can worry about your weight gain, get ulcers, suffer from high blood pressure, have a heart attack brought on by the stress of anxiety, and die early. Or you cannot worry about your weight gain, enjoy life, relax, and live until you are 107. Or in either case, be run over by a really, really, really fat guy driving a semi who can't reach the brakes because of his beer gut, in which case it really didn't make much difference in the final analysis what you did about your eating since what actually does matter is what the fat truck driver ate. And you can bet he pretty much ate whatever he wanted to. Maybe he'll send flowers to your widow...and enjoy a couple Big Macs to commemorate your demise.

I am working on another book at this very moment about my weight loss secrets, tentatively titled HOW TO SHED UGLY POUNDS WITHOUT LOSING WEIGHT, but until that invaluable volume comes along to save mankind, let me share just a couple ideas with you by way of relaxing the tension you have been getting from those television doctors who never seem to have any patients needing treatment. For example, always buy cookies and pies in small-town bakeries and cafes where they do their own baking because such products never come with nutrition labels, the main source of dietary anxiety and tension in America today. Also, if you are going to eat things like caramel nut rolls, ice cream bars, or chocolate fudge squares, do it at night, again when you are spared the discomfort of looking at those ugly and confrontational lists of ingredients, amounts of sugar, salt, and fat, and designations of portions…"This candy bar meets all governmental nutritional standards and contain only 75 calories per serving; approximate servings per two-ounce item = 182." America's problem is not bad nutrition, but too much information about nutrition. Reading all that stuff can make you nuts. Solution = don't read all that stuff.

You can also decrease anxiety resulting from that weight gain that is inevitable with ageing with small changes in your life style—always making a point for example of standing beside tank trucks, grain silos, dirigibles, elephants, 747s, and other things that make you look thin in comparison. Make a point whenever eating to be with someone who is a real pig; again, the comparison will make you look and feel downright moderate by comparison.

The importance of fashion should never be underestimated when it comes to avoiding NIMT (Nutrition-Induced Mental Trauma). People ask why I always wear overalls; my response is honest—"because they flatter the full-figured gent." Moreover, overalls have built-in expansion provisions in shoulder straps and side buttons that allow for additional emergency enlargements without going to a tailor's shop. I now wear suspenders rather than a belt (both when there is some jeopardy of either failing) and with the help of a good friend in Hawaii I now have a variety of colorful, 3XL Hawaiian shirts hanging in my closet. Generously cut, loose Hawaiian shirts.

Book store shelves groan under the weight of the hundreds of books revealing secrets to weight loss…protein, carbohydrates, aura reduction, liposuction, tap dancing, pilates, pirates, pyrites… and it's all bullshit. The only way to lose weight is to eat less and do more. There it is. Four words: eat less, do more. There are variations, of course, like DRINK less. That's always been the secret for me. I do like a cocktail now and then, or a martini, or a glass of good wine or good beer. Or bad wine or bad beer. And I have found that the moment I cut out the Happy Hour routine, I start losing weight. For that very reason, I have suggested that a sure way for people who are drinkers to lose weight is to quit drinking. Even if that doesn't help you live longer, it sure will make it seem like you are living longer.

What sense does it make when you know you are nearing the end of everything including breathing to give up one of the real joys of life? Any real joy of life? I have found that I can (and have) induced the unlikely spirit of…uh…what do they call it?…yeah that's it…<u>moderation</u> in my life by drinking only good stuff. The formula seems to be that a little really good stuff equals a lot of really bad stuff. For one thing, there is the price. I once sat at a living room table with a dear friend, in a wonderful home, and we sipped two Scotches that collectively cost $2100. You can understand that they were small sips. And damned few in number. You don't have to go that far. Nor to such expense. I really enjoy a good rye whiskey. And I have found that Old Grand-Dad and Jim Beam (I like even the much distained Old Overholt, frequently dismissed as "Old Overcoat") are drastically underestimated ryes…probably because there are not many rye drinkers left in this country. So while some might slop down six or eight whiskey sours from Kesslers or Ancient Age (don't get me wrong, those are might fine whiskeys too; I have enjoyed my share of them and if either distiller wants to change my preference, he should feel free to send me a case or two for quality control sampling), I have found enormous contentment in one (or at the most two) modest snifters of Grand-Dad or Jim Beam. I can roll a generous ounce around in a nice glass (although for some reason a campfire and tin cup seems to become a virtual garnish for rye whiskey) for an hour or so and just glow with joy. Thus, one can cut down on intake by moving up in quality, or perhaps cost. Or build a nice campfire and finding yourself a tin cup.

All joking aside (which isn't an easy step for me) if you would like to put another ten or twenty years on your life, find new vitality (and perhaps as one very fat friend of mine once noted after he lost a substantial amount of weight, "discover two inches you didn't know you had"), lose weight. I reached a weight I found so depressing I was cornered into following my own advice...eating less and working more...and lost 30+ pounds. The results were astonishing, even to me, and I live inside this frame, after all. I not only found that I had new energy, and had less trouble with sleep apnea, my knees which had become almost totally crippled were miraculously relieved and suddenly I was a different person. Still overweight, but substantially improved in my health and disposition.

Two results have come of this...first, since I am still overweight, I now want to lose more to see exactly where this leads. Maybe my dream of sleeping one night between Venus and Serena Williams still has a chance of being realized, and secondly, and this is really important for a guy like me who isn't all that excited about self-abuse, I never really deprived myself. I ate pretty much what I always ate, just...as I have said for so long in my dieting advice...less. As I ate less (but still of all the good stuff, please note), I was able to do more, and I did it. And as I ate less and did more, I lost more weight, and was able to do more. And eat a bit more, always of the good stuff. Not nutritionally good stuff but stuff I like...good bourbon, big burgers, mashed potatoes. It takes time and requires some minor self-control, but take it from this one old Geezer, it's worth it in terms of what it does for your life.

While we're on the topic, what's the deal with every blasted medication manufactured insisting that it must not be taken with alcohol? Why not make things easier on geezers and produce medications that are particularly effective when taken with a nice glass of wine, couple of bitter ales, or a snifter of good brandy?

Why not make life better instead of worse for someone who already needs medication, for Pete's sake? "Take one tablet after the evening meal…avoid using this medication while using alcohol." What idiot came up with <u>that</u> vision of The Golden Years? Offer instead a formulation that works best when combined <u>with</u> alcohol? How hard would that be? I'm no genius chemist but I have not a doubt in my mind that with about fifteen minutes work a chemist who graduated in the bottom of his class could produce this bit of pharmaceutical common sense.

# MISC HEALTH:

We all know that a washing machine inevitably gives out a week or two after the warranty expires. That's just the nature of things…a law of physics Newton would have come up with if he had had a washing machine. You will find in Geezerhood that your body pretty much does the same thing. I imagine I am going to get a lot of mail after this book comes out complaining that in my inventory of geezerly afflictions I have left out shin splints, shingles, gall bladder problems, strokes, liver spots, baldness, ear hair, toenail fungus (allegedly curable by the way with applications of the ever-useful WD-40… externally), and…well…all those wonderful physical events that are the landmarks of the hahahaha Golden Years. Believe me, I have been furiously upgrading these pages as in the year or so of writing them my inventory of afflictions and injuries has enlarged its variations…a scalded foot, a Pacemaker, an increasing ability to fall asleep in my recliner while at the same time finding it ever harder to sleep through a night.

No longer will you use an appointment with the oncologist as an excuse to have a nice meal and maybe a movie before you return home. Now you will start to bundle that trip to have your prostate exam with a stop by the clinic to have your blood tested, or maybe with the eye doctor to get a new eye glass prescription, or an appointment with the podiatrist have that funny little bump on your left little piggy looked at, or a check up with the dermatologist to get some skin tags whacked off. Or all of those things. Or more likely you will arrange a day of appointments with your urologist, oncologist, and a radiation treatment on the theory that this way you'll only have to drop your trousers once. Go ahead and laugh. It's the truth.

You will find you have a new fascination with home remedies, spurred in large part by the fact that your bill at the pharmacy has now moved to the top of your monthly expense sheet. You will actually pay attention to television ads for medications from stool softener to butt spackle, sometimes even TiVOing an especially evocative commercial and watching it in slow motion.

Some home cures seem to have a solid foundation in experimentation and discovery…for example, the application of WD-40 for just about everything from toenail fungus to head lice. Others seem more dubious but nonetheless enjoy enormous popularity and apparently have something to them, even though no one seems to know what that may be…for example, a bar of soap (Ivory being currently preferred…"it floats!") under one's sheets being a miracle cure for all manner of aches and pains.

This winter I have found my hands hurting more and more…arthritis?…and when I mentioned this to Linda, she said that she had heard "somewhere" that putting one's hands in hot, soapy water twice a day would work miracles on precisely this kind of problem. What's more, she offered me the use of her kitchen sink for my therapy. While I was there, she said, I could go ahead and do the dishes. After about a week of this I haven't detected any real difference but she assures me that if I keep it up another couple months, I may be surprised. She is a kind and generous woman, that Linda.

You will in fact find that one of the most interesting features of advanced seniority is the simultaneous increase of television advertisements applicable precisely to you and your afflictions. It's as if someone in an advertising firm is spying on you, somehow becoming aware of your every new problem from the poetically titled "erectile disfunction" to a wide variety of difficulties encountered in the bathroom, from excessive gas to leakage, from too little to too much of just about everything. And now that you are over 60, no one seems to have any shame about talking about such things with you. It gets to the point where you'd just as soon feel bad with the prospect of getting better than feel good and know that there's not a chance in hell this condition is going to last very long.

However, I am not even going to try to establish a complete inventory of all the gifts old age has given me or might bring to you. For one thing, there's not enough room in one book to list all that stuff. Secondly, it's quite enough—thank you—to consider the half dozen hazards and afflictions I have personally enjoyed that can hopefully serve as representative of the entire potential catalog. And third, I am not a physician or sickologist so all I can talk about with any sense of competence (not a factor, I realize, that gets in the way of most physicians or sickologists expressing their own bewilderment with certainty) is my experiences in watching this good old body of mine start to fray at the edges.

Whatever problems you encounter in your journey into Geezerdom, you will know that you have crossed over into that magic land when you realize that you no longer look for a cure…for things to get better…but simply want to hold on in hopes that things won't get any worse. You will come to think of that stasis as being good enough. It's a constant struggle day by day to get back to the morning's base line when you're a Geezer.

There are the ordinary afflictions of life, like a hernia, that can come along just about any time in the course of a life but which take on added emphasis in geezerhood. It takes longer to recover from even minor health problems and the mood seems to be, "Hey, as if I didn't have problems enough, now my bellybutton gasket is going bad too." Through all my life I have been anything but puny, and despite what it must sound like in this recitation of medical misadventures, I suspect that I am still healthier than most men. And I have borne those woes with more than usual courage, I like to think.

Not to mention that things take longer to heal when you're a geezer and once again there's that thing about all these kids with various certifications and fancy educations who now have some sort of official permission to humiliate you. Inevitably there are young women with names like Tiffany, Jennifer, Brandee, Camembare, and Shablee lathering up your groin, heaving your various equipages out of the way, and shaving away with cavalier inattention with a straight edge razor microhair widths from your most valued attributes while chatting about who they favor on "American Idol" or last night's surprises on "Desperate Housewives." I suspect by the time I am 90 years old, some teenybopper named Krystall will be flailing away at my pubic hair with a mini-mower while asking the doctor what <u>he</u> is wearing to the senior prom that night.

I have told you my theory about nurses entertaining themselves by inventing new ways to get to various parts of my body through the most unlikely possible entrances...which they pretty much create at random anyway. When I had my hernia repair, as I recall the nurse shaved the bottoms of my feet. I was under anesthesia of course so I can't say for sure whether she was just toying with me or they actually went in through that avenue, but do know that I wouldn't be the least bit surprised if the next time I go to my dentist to have my teeth cleaned, his nurse will invite me to lie flat on my stomach and to ...well... "open wide."

Which provides me an excellent segue into the two parts of the deteriorating senior body I would like to discuss next, the alpha and omega of it, the stem and the stern, both ends of the same long tube that constitutes the principal passage through one's being...the mouth and the...uh...the other end. There is, to be sure, a certain amusing irony in geriatric humor that one of the things that will be bringing you some of your physical problems is... the cure for other physical problems. Yes, that's right: many of the problems you are going to experience in your health will result from whatever is being done to treat other problems you are already experiencing. You have to admit, it is a kind of "I Love Lucy" situation.

For example, most of my life I've had pretty good teeth, my folks being generous and insistent that I drank my milk and avoided sweets. But on my last visit the dentist took one look and said...and this is a direct quote..., "Jeez, Rog...have you been eating rocks again?" Four broken teeth. In one six-month period I somehow broke four of my teeth. What could possibly have caused something like that, the dentist wondered, the rock-chewing tendency having been eliminated. He asked me about changes in diet, or maybe teeth gnashing in my sleep (hey, how would I know? I'm sleeping!), or accidents with jaw bumping involved. Curiously the dentist never brought up any questions about the potential that I'd been indulging in overly energetic sexual activities, also known (as I understand it) to the younger generation as "monkey sex," but as I explain below, I have some trouble keeping up with modern terminology. Not to mention other things. I just said something to Linda about how maybe we should try this "monkey sex" thing all the young people are talking about and she said, "You'll have to get yourself a monkey." This leads me to believe I maybe on the wrong track here, either about monkeys or about sex. Or both. But no, I couldn't think of anything I had participated in along those lines...but...wait a minute...when I was at some stage of my prostate cancer treatments...something was said about radiation weakening bone structures...but nothing about teeth. That, the dentist said, could be it. The cure for my one problem...cancer... had brought with it another problem...broken teeth. Terrific.

Yes, another instance of a cure that treats a problem while at the same time inducing a half dozen others. You take Coumadin for your heart problems...and then need regular blood tests because of the problems caused by that particular poison being introduced into your system. Radiation works on the cancer...and maybe a bunch of other noninvolved parts too, so you'll need that

Citrucel. And Imodium. And glycerin suppositories. (No, those are not candles and need not be lit to be activated.)

My own rear differential, if you catch my drift, started showing signs of bad design fairly early on. I'd guess the problems stem from the occupational hazards resulting from doing most of my work whilst sitting. To begin with, the most challenging problem of hemorrhoids is how to spell it. Is there a more ridiculous word in the English language? I mean, jeez, as if it weren't hard enough to talk about a serious physical affliction that inevitably causes gales of laughter rather than waves of sympathy, it has to be hemher...uh, hemmoroi...er, hehmmerho.... Piles.

And then you consider that everything that is going to happen in regard to this fairly personal problem is going to happen behind your back.... It's just not a good arrangement at all. And again, the "cure" is an operation that converts what was a minor discomfort to a major agony... that is to say, the removal of the tape they use to hold your cheeks apart while the doctors work their magic on your catalytic converter, which is to say, the removal of long and wide strips of hair from your as-it-were seat cushion. And in my case, sitting as I do about an inch above any chair seat on a well lofted cushion of heinie hair (I know—more than you really wanted to know), that involved something akin to clear cutting the forest lands of the State of Washington.

I am something of a blabbermouth, this book being an excellent example. I try to honor other people's privacy but somehow manage to overshare, as my daughter phrases it, when it comes to my own personal matters. So, when I had my vent pinked, as it were, I shared the experience and my complaints with my friends around our morning work-place coffee table. Two days later one of them showed up and made a formal and public presentation to me of a new prosthesis, a mechanical, stainless steel, chromed rectum prosthesis. I probably would be rich now if I had taken the idea and run with it, but considering my condition at the moment there wasn't much running to be done. This metal device my friend made for me has a reverse and barbed flange to prevent inadvertent loss of the device and a metal door with a spring that slams shut decisively and firmly when released. One thing for sure, there'd be no more need for operations with scissors, scalpels, and sutures if I installed this device…just an occasional touch up with a bur grinder and grease gun. (The circle of my friends privy—as it were—to the design of my metal butt muffler did decide that any future models of our pooper prosthesis should definitely include a zirk style lubrication fitting.)

Being an inventive lot, we instantly conceived of improvements and additions to the basic model of The Mark I Mechanical Anus our friend had fabricated for me. For example, we agreed that the first alteration would as a matter of course be to thread the inside of the device, thus allowing the easy installation of a muffler. Or for festive occasions…a whistle! Or, how about a camera-like iris so the wearer could stop down to f-12 or f-16 on those days when time is not an issue or throw open the gates, so to speak, to f1.2 when there is no time for dallying? And if you weren't just thoroughly disgusted by that image, how about the notion of changeable templates screwing into the rear-end fitting that would create festive underwear imprints… shamrocks for St. Patrick's Day, a bunny for Easter, a Santa or Christmas tree for that holiday, and of course…something pyrotechnic for the Fourth? As I recall, my buddies and I had way too much time on our hands those days.

I still take great pleasure when we have visitors and the conversation turns to geriatric problems and then to anus failures…and what conversation doesn't eventually go that route when you're over 60 years of age?!…in saying "Anybody want to see my asshole?" Whereupon I run upstairs and return with this chromed prototype of my anal prosthesis. When one gets older, one's humor turns to such desperation.

Speaking of desperation, what the heck is it with depression these days? Am I the only person around here with sufficient endorphins or flavenoids or adenoids or solenoids or whatever the hell it is that is missing in everyone I know, causing them permanent and profound blue funks? Am I missing something? I think life is great. I figure I've been dealt with more than fairly. I see funny stuff going on that makes me laugh all the time. What makes other people sob uncontrollably puts me in a state of hysterical laughter. What's that all about? It seems like everyone in my family and everyone I know is depressed to the point of suicide or at least collapse. (When I express my bewilderment about this, Linda says, "Hmmmm…everyone around you is plunged into desperate depression…. And what is it they all have in common?")

At any rate, while I can't claim that I understand depression, not having experienced it, I can say that I know the ripple effect this accursed plague of gloom has on everyone around it, and it's not good. As I tell them, I'm 100% German so whenever I feel a little depressed, I just think about invading some a small, helpless country and suddenly I feel good again. Depression? No, thanks…I'm German. It's never hard to sympathize with the afflictions of others, even harder when it's something with invisible triggers like depression. I know for a fact you can't simply talk someone out of depression by reminding them how lucky they are, which is a real problem when you are struggling with cancer to stay alive while they are trying to figure out a way to end theirs. You might just as well try to talk your household plumbing out of this silliness of springing a leak. It won't work. So, here's one place I don't have a lot of encouragement to offer, having only seen this Black Horror second hand.

I do have the impression however that even people with chronic depression aren't depressed when they have something really going wrong in their lives. That is, when you are really unhappy about something you don't have much time or energy to be unhappy about something else. I have no idea what is going on in this world that clinical depression now seems to be endemic but I think that what we need to eradicate it is another Great Depression. Do what you can. Vote Republican. Then everyone will be happy again because we'll all be equally miserable. I think that's how that works.

I'm pretty certain the need to laugh when afraid, or even just troubled, is particularly important to men. We just don't like to sit down and have a serious conversation with a doctor about stuck bowels, uncooperative wienies, or even bad teeth. We'd much rather have a buddy who is a mechanic or plumber commiserate and laugh with us. No kidding, that makes us feel better than actually treating the problem medically. At this very moment I have a friend who has just gone through the trauma of being diagnosed with prostate cancer and then undergoing the very serious operation of having his prostate removed, the possible consequences being even worse than the original problem. You think I'm kidding? How about having to wear a belt with your poop draining into it the rest of your life? Or total impotence? Or still having cancer even after all that trouble? Or just dying?

But I knew he was on the road to recovery when I told him I was having trouble finding a publisher for this book and that Lovely Linda thinks it might be my working title, GOLDEN YEARS MY ASS! He suggests alternative titles…"As Your Pecker Droops So Are the Days of Our Lives," for example. Or "Do You Need a Director for the Erector of Your Pecker?" Or "The New Penal Code Book for the Old Penal System." Or "A Penis Saved Is a Penis Earned." First, that is the way a man deals with medical problems. Second, that's the way a man <u>recovers</u> from a medical problem.

I can only hope I'm not letting you down with such a short list of the physical and medical problems I have experienced in my journey through Geezerland. I almost wish I had a lot more things wrong with me so I would have a longer narrative to offer you. I told Linda that I felt I was running short of physical failings to write about and she said that maybe I'd get lucky and catch something else serious before I finished this book. But no, I feel fine, thank you.

Just getting old takes its toll even when the afflictions have no fancy names. I have increasing trouble buttoning those little buttons on my shirt cuffs and so sometimes Linda helps me fasten them. I asked her a few days ago if that makes her feel that she is stuck with an old man. She said we'd know when we reached that stage when she started sewing Velcro closers on my shirt sleeves. And tying my gloves on string passed through the sleeves of my chore coat. And when there was nothing left by the door but shoes that can be slipped off and on without fussing with shoestrings.

Even if you don't enjoy specific physical afflictions with fancy names and expensive treatments or medications, there is a kind of creeping geezerness that can't be outflanked. If nothing else, as you get older you will find things simply slowing down. You may recognize this transition in language if not in action. For example, a "jackrabbit start" in the morning will mean only that you don't wear your pajamas to lunch. And "lunch" will come to mean a sandwich, soup, a bowl of pills that looks for all the world like a generous helping of M & Ms, and a half-hour nap. Happy hour comes earlier and earlier until it falls sometime around noon; a friend once educated me that we don't have to worry about drinking before noon because before noon, a cocktail is officially a "restorative." "Bedtime" will slowly but surely move from eleven o'clock to ten thirty and then ten. "Staying up and raising a little hell" will eventually signify that you were awake for the opening of "Saturday Night Live." Or most of it anyway. Your wife will occasionally wake you out of a sound sleep just to make sure you're not dead. Presuming you're not. Bedtime migrates to nine o'clock and then eight. Pretty soon you're putting on your 'jammies before the evening news. And eventually as the time you get going in the morning and the time of day when you start to close things down get ever closer and closer to each other, you'll begin to wonder if it's really worth the trouble of taking off those pajamas since you're going to be putting them back on again before they even have a chance to reach room temperature in the interim.

Part of this problem in my case was a severe case of apnea… the absolute proof against the nonsense of intelligent design if there ever was one. Apnea is when you are asleep and forget to breathe. And once you've been breathing for quite some time, like 70 years, it becomes a real habit, and a habit I should note that you don't want to break. I hadn't noticed…I was always sleeping at the time…but Linda told me that I would stop breathing for what seemed like a half hour or so at a time and then suddenly gasp for breath. All night, every night. No wonder I was getting up in the morning still exhausted.

We went to a bunch of doctors, who as usual had no idea what they were talking about. They recommended an operation, which would have solved their problem about how to send their kids to an expensive Eastern college that autumn. They finally decided I should go for "tests" to Torquemada's Sleep Clinic. At a sleep clinic, they stick wires and sensors all over you, put you on a hard, strange bed in a room with lots of peculiar noises and bright lights, watch you all night, and then come to the remarkable conclusion that, gosh, you don't seem to sleep very comfortably. And what you need is one of their $500 machines that fits on your face like a snorkel mask and forces air into your lungs on a regular basis while condensing your breath and dripping the slimy, cold, goo back onto your face all night long. At which point you will find that your condition is worse. At which point they will decide they really need to sell you more of their magic goat-gland potions.

I'd rather die. No kidding, it is that bad. But once I broke free of the shaman practitioners, I figured it all out on my own: I lost a mess of weight and the problem was solved. Not only did that treatment cost me nothing, it saved me about $500 a week on McDonald's fast foods.

The perfume of Ben Gay will replace the scented Kama Sutra oils of your youth. The daily dose of Citrucel will be seen as a blended frappe. You will no longer think of a "marital aid" as being a tube of KY Jelly but the off switch on your hearing aid. And the idea of enjoying a "saucy little tart" will mean only a generous helping of rhubarb pie. A la mode.

Not only will your own linguistic usages change but you will find that words you still use no longer have the same meanings you have always thought they had...young people will find your indignation bewildering when you react to phrases like "He really screwed me," or "Man, does that ever suck." Perfectly good words in your vocabulary become the stuff of giggles and confusion: "typewriter," "hi-fi," or "carburetor" come to my mind.

A couple days ago I was discussing my brilliant idea discussed later in these pages for a perfect geezer retirement home with Linda and Antonia. I noted that aside from a myriad of other wonderful perks I would include to make male elders absolutely delighted with their seniority, once or twice a week a cleaning lady would come in and tidy up each apartment...oh... something along the line of a gorgeous, young Vietnamese lady (Southeast Asian women have to be the most gorgeous women in the world...aside from Linda and her sisters, that is to say)... naked. For one thing, that would cut down on expenses for uniform for the help. It would also make living worthwhile. I mentioned that a friend...I won't mention his name to protect the guilty...suggested that we name this establishment something that would suggest some of these perks...maybe, oh, Cooters...you know...like Hooters...except for coots. Well, I thought that was hilarious, and even thought about something like The Cooterie.

Daughter Antonia went white. Her jaw fell open. "Daaaaaad," she said in visible horror. "Never say that word again!"

What? "Geezer?" "Coot?" "Hooters?" "Perks?"

"No. That...that...that other word...."

"Cooter?"

The air exploded from her lungs and she almost swooned to the floor except that young people don't even know what "to swoon" means these days yet to be able to do one. "Yes...that word...never say it again. It's...it's...it's FILTHY!"

So, it's all right to say, oh, "That sucks," but not okay to say "Girls have cooties?"

Antonia's knees buckled and she leaned on the table for support. "I told you never to say that word again!"

Linda and I looked at each other in amazement. "Well, isn't that the berries?" Linda said in a hushed tone…and then, with her usual perfect timing, "'Berries' isn't a dirty word now too, is it?"

If you should overhear a conversation between younger people…presuming you have the capacity for hearing anything at all yet <u>over</u>hearing anything…you may suspect they are speaking in some kind of code: "bits" and "bytes" have nothing to do, it turns out, with food, for example. I once used the word "hifi" in a crowd of youngsters and from the general hilarity you'd have thought I told a terrific joke. No one uses the word "hifi" any more, it seems, or for that matter "stereo." I was, the young people told me, three or four linguistic waves behind in my sound system terminology. I don't even try any more. What's an iPod? I have no idea. And what is WiFi? Or a Wii? Does "whiz" still mean the same thing I think it does? You find even terms like "Walkman" under the "Electronic Antiques" category on eBay. I have not a clue what a "Blackberry" is or does. I might just as well be talking about an Edison phonograph when I try to find out what's going on with music reproduction these days. No kidding, a couple evenings ago there was a television commercial where one guy trying to sell some sort of telephone was taunting another because his outmoded, obsolete, perfectly imperfect hand-held whatever telephone could only…brace yourself because you're going to have a hard time believing what I'm about to say…isn't good for anything but… <u>making telephone calls</u>! You couldn't even grate carrots or catch fish with this lump of electronic crap! At least that's what he was telling me. I'm not only behind the technological curve, I spun out, hit the curbing, and went over the cliff years ago.

I went through a couple dozen mid-life crises during my life. I went to grand prix racing school, traveled above the Arctic Circle in northern Greenland, spent some time snorkeling the reefs off the Yucatan, took some road trips with buddies, sang "Good Vibrations" on stage with the Beach Boys, had some flings in my between-marriages bachelor years, got a couple tattoos, and even ate snails. But MID-life crises are no longer a big deal because a lot has been written and said about MID-life crises. On the other hand, no one has had much to say about LATE-life crises.

Midlife crises become geriatric crises almost without transition, one just oozing into the other. But senior moments (as lapses of memory are so often called these days) are less often daring-do than daring-don't. All these years you've been working and saving so you can eventually do all those things you've always wanted to do and now that you can…you can't. I left my last real job when I was fifty years old and then found out the rude reality that when you don't have a real job, you can't retire. Hell, when you don't have a real job, you don't even get vacations or weekends off! What's worse, people start to presume that since you don't have a job, you also don't have anything to do, which is precisely the opposite of the reality of the matter. When you don't have a job, you're always busy. It's like living in a small town where "there's nothing going on and nothing to do." You're so darn busy, you scarcely have a second to yourself to think!

So, if you don't have a job, either before or after whatever landmark you use to determine retirement, you are constantly bombarded by visitors, people dropping by for coffee or a chat, folks needing a hand doing something, well-wishers coming through to make sure you aren't sitting around bored…when all you really want is a few minutes to yourself so you can get something done! A couple weeks ago I was jarred into a cruel reality when I got a letter from a friend notifying me that I was going to be his vacation destination for the summer and he'd be dropping by to spend a few days just sitting on my back porch with me to help me pass the time. I marked DECEASED on the envelope and sent it back by express mail in hopes of heading him off before he loaded up the RV and headed my way. The hahahahahaha Golden Years are bad enough without you becoming a vacation destination.

# SOLUTIONS:

Now, after all that whining and bellyaching, here's the bottom line: The hahahahaha Golden Years actually aren't all that bad. In fact, I'm having a pretty good time of it despite the occasional glitch in the hitch. You know the old story about the guy banging his head against the brick wall because it feels so good when he stops…well, old age is a lot like that. Every new problem that comes along has the advantage of reminding me that things could be worse, and there's considerable hope that they will be better. Besides, what's the alternative?

As a result, I find myself now enjoying some very small things that completely escaped my attention when I was a lot younger and a lot busier. No kidding, starting sometime in April every year and right through until late September, I wake up every morning not just smiling but downright laughing. Why? Because I have learned to recognize and appreciate the thoroughly goofy and insanely inventive morning song of the brown thrasher that makes a habit of starting his day outside my bedroom window. And when a chorus of coyotes comes through our bottom ground and cuts loose with some highly ornamented aria from something by some minor rococo composer, I am never upset anymore about being awakened. Even if I can't get right back to sleep, I lie there and take comfort knowing that by golly, if those wonderful rascals can survive the warfare being waged against them with semi-automatic rifles with long-range scopes, poison, traps, all-terrain vehicles, and even airplanes, then there's surely hope for us geezers. And besides...I can sleep as late as I want to now. And then spend some time sitting out on the patio blinking in the sun. Kind of like Mr. Coyote Himself, come to think about it.

There are advantages to getting older...not many, to be sure, but you have to make of them what you can since everything else seems to go to hell. You are first to get the annual flu shots at the clinic, for example, and there are all those discounts on hotels, airlines, and even fast foods. There was a time when tears of joy came to my eyes when a store clerk would ask to see my identification card to make sure I was old enough to get into a naughty movie or buy alcohol. But now...here's a hint for young ladies who want <u>really</u> big tips when serving Geezers: when you are dealing with guys like me, start things off by saying, "I'm sorry, sir, we cannot give you that discount. It's for seniors only. There's no way you are over 60 years old. I'll have to see two forms of photo i.d." Stand back when you try this, however, because along with the big tip, the old coot is liable to make a jump for you or grab for your fanny. There are a lot of old-timers like me that figure we just can't pass up a chance like that.

Once you're past 60 or 70 years old you will also find that you wind up with a lot more plaques. After my bout with prostate cancer, I started collecting a plaque, award, or trophy every couple of weeks. People figured there was a pretty good chance of me dying so if they were going to say something nice, they probably better get it in pretty soon. After the tests came back that my blood showed that we had probably beaten the Big C (in fact, my doctor says that my blood turned out to be about 49% piss and 49% vinegar) I didn't tell many people because I was so enjoying all the tributes to my contributions the general welfare. I guess people figured I must be about to cash in my chips so they jumped in to give me a cheap plaque and a round of applause before it was too late to be included in the will. Sometimes I wish I had thought of this whole mortality and death threat thing earlier.

Curiously, in Geezerhood one begins to take a different view of the occasion of waking up. It is one thing—an unpleasant thing—to be awakened by an alarm at six or seven in the morning and then to have to get to a job by eight or nine. It's enough to make you grumpy. On the other hand, when you don't have a job to get up for, things take on a totally new aspect. It is wonderfully pleasant to wake up at your leisure at, oh, six or seven in the morning. And then enjoy the morning as you get cracking on your latest project by…say…maybe, oh, eight or nine.

Besides, you don't have to just sit there and take it. There's something you can do about the ageing process. And I sure as billy hell don't mean something stupid like a face-lift. Where do people get the notion that plastic surgery makes them look like anything other than some pathetic old fool who got plastic surgery? Some old farts who are ageing ungracefully get parts readjusted, reroofed, reupholstered, relined, repacked, respackled, whatever, and then croak from their bionic bodies how much better they feel now that they "look better." Honey, take it from me…you may feel better after all that surgical redecorating and landscaping on your face and body but there isn't any way on God's green earth that you look better! Besides, the few experiences I have had with surgery pretty much convince me that there's no way I'm about to go under the knife by choice, no matter what it promises to do for my turkey-gobbler throat. No way.

Running around with kids and acting like a kid won't help either. Neither does wearing the kind of clothing kids are wearing. You can be rock-solid sure you're simply not going to bring it off and will wind up looking stupid. Neither will wearing what passes for official Geezer clothing… Double-knit burgundy golfing pants tucked up around your nipples with a white patent leather belt matching the white shoes you're wearing over argyles does <u>not</u> say "I'm old and proud of it." It says, "I may be old but as you can see, I really haven't learned all that much over the years." Just dress the way you always have and that way fewer people will notice that anything dramatic...like old age...has changed about you. That's the theory behind my wearing overalls. I've always worn overalls and I always will. They make me look old? And out-of-date? So what? I <u>am</u> old. And I am quite content being out of date, thank you very much.

Local communities these days go out of their way to provide entertainment and assistance for the elderly, but it's almost never what the elderly would arrange for themselves, given half a chance. Where do activity directors in retirement homes get the idea that all old people find accordion music attractive, for example? Everyone my age is a superannuated hippie. Polka music, hell. Make it Jimi, Mick, or Janis, with maybe something by new up-and-comers like Z Z Top or Lynyrd Skynnyrd.

One community near here put together a senior citizen center with lots of activities...macramé workshops, seminars on good colon health, speakers on how to make arrangements for distributing your organs when you kick off, fun things like that. How about bringing in some strippers? That would be fun for everyone, probably even the strippers. Or instead of bringing in yet another junior high school swing choir with yet another of those tired, canned routines, why not make the kids sit down and listen to geezer stories about the war for a change? Any war. It doesn't matter.

Anyway, this town nearby had a senior citizen center with activities the Baptists thought would be fun. And over at the town tavern, the bartender finally got tired of working all day hauling coffee at a quarter a cup to a table of grumpy Geezers playing Pitch, so he threw them out of his establishment. So the Geezers in the town got together and organized their own activities center where they could do what they damn well pleased...always a good plan for Geezers anyway. They play cards there, and argue politics, and while I don't know for sure, I can only hope they occasionally spring for a nice, wholesome, and firm young stripper (you know...younger than 50) to come in and remind them of the good old days...dancing not to Whoopee John and his accordion but Z Z Top banging out "Nationwide." You can get some notion of the old-timers' attitude and idea of what a good time is by what they dubbed their social hall... "The Dead Peckers Club." Now tell me--what stripper wouldn't kill to play that venue just for the fun of it, even if her g-string had to have a little pocket sewn onto it to collect and hold the quarters?

My mother lived for some time not far from us in a very nice retirement home apartment. It was clean, convenient, and safe. The food was good, there were all kinds of services available to her, and she was quite happy there. It was perfect. For a woman. I'm not sure I'd be all that enthusiastic about it as a man. But being the kind of guy who comes up with solutions and doesn't just whine and moan about problems, I have decided to start working on the perfect retirement home for Geezers. I have talked this over with some friend, notably my old buddy Mick, approaching Geezerhood himself, and we are getting darn near enthusiastic about this idea, suggesting there might be something worth looking forward to in our hahahahahahahaha Golden Years.

Mom's apartment set-up was quite nice in that each unit had an outdoor exit onto a patio. A Geezerly retirement home would have that too because you'd need a place to have your barbecue, and if you front on the part of the home that faces the lake or river, you could even set up your duck blind or fishing dock right outside your patio door. When Mom left her apartment, for example to go to dinner, she exited into a hall and across that hall from her door was the door to her garage area. She didn't drive any more so she used the garage for storage, and that would be the idea in Geezerville too: each unit would come with a "garage," which would be each gentleman's woodworking shop, party room, tractor repair shop, comic book collection storage area, wine-making room...you know, whatever it is that this particular geezer enjoys.

The food at my ideal Home for Geezers would be man food... spareribs, jerky, big greasy hamburgers, chilidogs, sardines and crackers..stinky stuff mostly. No salads or fancy desserts. Ice cream, pie, chocolate cake. No mousses, frappes, dinky dainties. No Jello allowed. No tapioca. Large curd cottage cheese only. Screw nutrition myths. Forget presentation and fancies. Forget manners. Silverware and dishes would be optional since real men eat mostly with their fingers and off their knees. Big screen TVs in the dining area would be constantly tuned to ESPN, Court TV, or the Playboy Channel. You could wear anything you want any time, including at meals, including nothing but underwear, pajamas, or overalls. You could wash your hands before you eat, or not. There'd be a shooting range of course and a library of manly reading...all my books for darn sure.

I have mentioned the important feature of our cleaning staff... naked, young ladies. Same with the serving staff in the dining area. And the bar maids in the lounge area...you know, the one with the free bar that opens at 10 a.m. ("Hey...it's noon in the Azores!") The bar would be stocked according to the tastes of the residents, and smugglers would keep the humidors stocked with Cuban Cohiba cigars. Dogs would be encouraged and in addition to the dogs kept by individual residents, there would be a couple institution labs...black, yellow, and chocolate...constantly available for petting, smelling doggy, and comforting to the guys with geriatric grumps.

I can't help but think back on an occasion when Jim Harrison, famous novelist and friend, was here in Dannebrog, my little town. He noticed that the town filling station was closed and up for sale. He looked it over and fantasized, "You know, Rog, we should buy this place and open the perfect eatery. Where the service bays are we would have the dining area.... Nothing but the very best of cuisine. There'd be no menu, no decisions to make. You just come in, sit down, and enjoy. Everything would be the very best food. In here, where the tire repair area is, we would have a stock of the best tools available...Snap-On,

Craftsman, that kind of thing… And there would be maybe an old car or tractor to work on. In the middle, where the office is now, would be the kitchen.

"You would sit down at the table and a gorgeous, naked, young woman [perhaps, dear reader, you are beginning to sense a pattern developing here] would bring you your salad and bread…nothing but absolutely perfect food. Perfectly gorgeous young women…you know, it's cloth that carries germs, so that's why they'd have to be naked. And when you finished your salad and bread…real, French butter, of course…you would drift over to the tool and tractor bay, work a while on the tractor, talk, maybe sip a good aperitif… Then back to the dining area where another gorgeous, young… naked… woman would bring your soup. Then back to the tools and repair work. When you and the entrée are quite ready, back to the dining area…and yet another gorgeous, naked, young woman…"

Jim stopped in mid-reverie. "But you know, Rog, as sure as you would try to start up a place like that, sooner or later….they'd make you open it to the public."

They'd probably do the same thing with my Ideal Geezer Retirement Home.

I have presented this plan as one for geezers…guys… guysers, as it were, but I have suspicions we need similar establishments for women. A lot of women are, to all appearances, human beings. And why is it that so many of the institutions designed for the care of the elderly have fallen into the hands of prudes, prims, prigs, Puritans, pompous, and pushy? The management and staff at my mother's last retirement home presumed…pre-diddlydamn-sumed!… that everyone would want to sit around eating tapioca and listening to hymns played on an accordian. So the prunes ruled. And Mom was indignant and bored. My buddy Mick was once working on some masonry on the grounds of a retirement home and occasionally an elderly gent came ambling out to check out his work, chat about manly things like fishing and brick laying, to talk man-talk, and…whatever. One day a stern guard…uh, caretaker came sniffing out to where Mick was working and started asking him questions, explaining that the old man in her charge almost surely had a bottle stashed somewhere on the grounds and just might have used his forays out to visit Mick as a means of escaping her oppression long enough to get a little sip of the wonderful warm, soothing bourbon he maybe had stacked under a rock or behind a tree. Mick told her he didn't know anything about that but has but forever regretted not telling that harridan to leave the old guy alone, to quit making his life miserable, to let him have his good whiskey now and again and at least a moment of pleasure in the final years—or days-- of his life. What business was it of this woman's where the old man found his comfort and joy? None. None!

Well, my mother sure was no drinker. But now and again through her 96 years of life she loved a half teaspoon of Kalhua in her coffee. She probably didn't drink a half pint in the entirety of her life. So when she one day told me from her hospice bed in the hospital, where she had gone to die, that she sure would like some Kalhua for her coffee, what do you think I did? For an instant I did wonder if there might be some bad interaction with her medications… again that stupid thing about medicines not being taken with alcohol…or maybe even without the medicines it just wouldn't be good for her. But then good sense set in. She was there to die, for God's sake! At the time we thought she had weeks to live. All she asked in this world aside from the company of her family was a half teaspoon of a good taste in her miserable hospital coffee. You damn right I'll get you some Kalhua, Mom! And I did. I bought her one of those little airline bottles of Kalhua and sneaked it past the guard towers and sentries and into her room. (I can only hope the statute of limitations has run on my crime of wanting to please my mother in her final hours.) Her delight was electric. She instantly rang her nurse-call and asked for a cup of coffee. When it arrived I spilled maybe a quarter ounce into her coffee. She sipped it, closed her eyes, and heaved a deep sigh of satisfaction. She handed me her cup and said sweetly, "More!"

Over that week she polished off her ounce or two of contraband liqueur and then worried about how she was going to dispose of the empty. Of course I would take it out when I left but just to joke I suggested that she toss it out her hospital window. "No," she laughed seditiously. "I have a better idea. I'll flip it out the window and over under Verna's window so they'll think it's hers!"

When we moved her to the room where she died, I asked her what she would tell them if they found her Kalhua stash and asked her about it. "I'll tell them it was here when I came," she said, having obviously thought about the plot well before she needed to.

I say "Screw the prigs." Enough of the Puritanism. Serve cocktails in hospitals, retirement homes, rest homes, and nursing homes. Why should joy die before the patient?

I don't know what to say about nursing homes. I don't like to think about nursing homes. No one does. It's one thing to live in a community of elderly people but quite another to be put into storage in a "full-care" facility where you are essentially in a holding pattern for clearance to land in that great airport in the sky, if you catch my drift. From this point, still hopefully a few years out, I am like just about everyone else I know and mumble "I'd rather be dead," which always seems like a good idea until you are just about dead, it seems. I have the feeling that even some folks in that situation would just as soon wave goodbye to the kids and be on their way. Life in any condition at all gets pretty close to no life at all. Or worse, life without life.

My buddy Woodrow and his siblings took their parents off the farm because they were worried about something happening to them out there so far removed from health care, virtually isolated during winter storms, where they were contacted only once or twice a day by telephone. The "kids," trying to do the right thing, put them into a very nice, sanitary nursing home with some wonderful new friends and healthful, nutritious meals. Rather than in the dusty, dirty old farmhouse where they had lived for sixty years, around old friends…like old tractors, a barn, cats and dogs, eating foods they were accustomed to and enjoyed, sleeping in their own beds, seeing the things they had known and loved all their lives. How wonderfully thoughtful!

Well, it wasn't a month before the old coots grabbed their walkers and made a slow-motion break-out. It took almost an hour for them to make it down the hall to the exit door, and then another half hour to get across the parking lot to their old pickup truck. Thank God, they didn't kill anyone on their long, looooong drive back out to the farm.

It took just a little while for the family to figure out what had happened and where Granny and Grandpa had gone. There was some trepidation when they approached the old farmhouse because no one could be sure the old folks were willing to be taken back into captivity alive. My buddy Woodrow finally talked some sense into his sibs and they decided that no matter how much longer their parents might live in a nursing home, if they did indeed live longer, they were scarcely doing them a favor. The choices were 1) a truly miserable life... perhaps prolonged even longer and thus inflicting more misery, or 2) a comfortable and happy life leading to a peaceful passing precisely where they wanted to be. Not where the kids wanted them to be.

And just two days ago I got an e-mail from another friend whose father was seriously ill and in a nursing facility. He had earlier sent me a photo of the old coot surrounded by his family... a kind of final family portrait... an oxygen tube up his nose, in a hospital gown, with all manner of medical machinery around him and hooked up to him. One thing I can say in favor of the otherwise situation—an absolutely stunning Oriental nurse was standing there too, taking his pulse, which almost surely was accelerating since looking at her picture was making my pulse speed up, and I was just looking at the photo. The old gent was about to begin a long and painful series of radiation treatments, a long (perhaps permanent) stay in the hospital, a pretty dreary final act to an otherwise completely satisfactory life.

But then I got this new, short note yesterday…telling me that the old goat had gone over the wall…with his 85-year-old girlfriend! And they had run off to Las Vegas to be married. And hopefully to have one hell of a good time, enjoy each other's company, fool around a little even, do some hooha-ing, spend the children's inheritance on prime rib dinners and fancy hotel suites with hot tubs and revolving round beds, stay up and gamble until, oh, ten p.m., maybe even take in some crazy stage show like Tom Jones… Damn the torpedoes! Full speed ahead, I say! (I got another report today: they are back from their elopement and very happy. Gramps called my buddy and asked him to pick him up and take him to the doctor for his treatments…and get him something to eat because he was hungry. Moral of this story: You can have cancer and be miserable…or you can have cancer and find some joy in life nonetheless.)

An extreme example of this was told to me by another friend 40 years ago, and his narrative has haunted me ever since. I suppose in my wildest dreams I see it as something of a template to be used in formulating my own final years or days. This friend was telling me about his grandparents back in Louisiana and how they lived a very quiet life in a small town, living in a small modest apartment above a flower shop run by the lady of the house. The couple managed to lead a good if unexciting life on her income from the shop and their social security.

Almost as an aside…he may have been a trifle uncertain about how we would react to the story…my friend then continued tentatively that they hadn't always lived within such modest means. No, the man had accumulated quite a fortune, actually…in oil. He had taken a lot of risks, worked like a dog, saved his money, been smart with his investments, followed the life of a solid citizen. His wife had always wanted a flower shop and so for one anniversary he bought her a little shop in a town actually too small for a flower shop. But, you know, it was more of a hobby and a gift of love rather than an actual business decision, investment, or commercial venture.

But one day well into his retirement, at a family gathering, a discussion had started among the children about how his estate would eventually be handled. The conversation grew a bit warm, and then hot, contentious and then confrontational, as the children made it clear who should be in charge, how the estate should be divided, who deserved the most, and who should be cut out of the will if there were any justice at all in this world. The old man watched all this but didn't have much to add to the discussion and no one bothered to ask him. The family gathering broke up almost in warfare and everyone went their own furious way.

A few weeks later the old man disappeared. He simply was nowhere to be found. His big Cadillac was gone from the garage, which wasn't all that unusual, but he didn't come home that night, nor the next morning. His wife called the law and they began some basic, routine checking and found that...uh-oh!...his accounts at the bank had also been drawn on to the point where there was only enough left for basic living necessities for his wife. It didn't seem that a kidnapper, con man, or extortionist would be that considerate so the law enforcement investigators had to leave open the possibility that as unlikely as it might seem, this quiet, prosperous, apparently happily retired and financially comfortable senior citizen had...run off on his own.

Almost a year later he came back, hitchhiking on the highway into town, bedraggled, broke, dissipated, exhausted... As the story eventually came out, he had indeed left on his own and taken all his resources except what it took for his wife...and now himself...to live on in the little apartment above the flower shop. Not only was he not ashamed or shy about revealing what he had done, he wanted to make it quite clear because he saw it all as something of a morality play.

He had given some considerable thought to the argument within his family and among his children about how they were going to divvy up his estate and spend his money. And he decided to save them all a lot of trouble by not leaving them anything to fight over. He had taken his money to Las Vegas, rented a penthouse apartment, stocked it with great potables from French wines to rare single-malt Scotches, held regular all-night séances with three, four, sometimes as many as six or eight naked showgirls, ordered up all the prime rib, champagne, caviar, pate, lobster, and shrimp they or he could hold, gambled and went to shows he'd always wanted to see, and generally carried on a debauch that any red-blooded male would envy. Until he ran out of money. And then he went home.

My friend was silent a moment after he finished his story about his grandfather. Then he said that none of the children ever talked with the old geezer again, an unexpected benefit of his flight of fancy-free. While the mother of the family did take him back in, she was never quite as warm as she had been previously. And the old man was the talk, joke, and scandal of the little town as he sat on his rocker on the second-floor porch above the flower shop the rest of his life, sunning himself in the Louisiana sun. And curiously, despite all of this, the old man never again was seen without a smile on his face. Isn't there a song about what treasures memories are? I think that's what the old coot was probably humming to himself as he sat there in the sun rocking.

Of course these are grand schemes. Who has the money to build the perfect Geezer retirement home I dream of? It wouldn't be cheap. So I have thought up some alternatives that would be much more manageable economically and yet still make major contributions to the condition of American Geezers. For example, my own invention, the Geezer Make-A-Wish Foundation. I think the Make-A-Wish Foundation for kids is a wonderful idea but, well, kids…. There is always hope and either there are cures for many of the curses that afflict children or the hope that there will be cures. But there's no cure for old age. When you reach 74 years of age as I have, you don't blithely chirp, "Well, the rest of my life is still ahead of me." Sure, the rest of your life is indeed ahead of you but that "rest" gets smaller every day and doesn't show much hope of improvement or cure. So why isn't there a modest Make-A-Wish Foundation for us old guys? It wouldn't need to involve a lot of money. Surely there are hundreds, maybe thousands, even millions of lovely younger women (younger at my age being somewhere less than 60, after all) who would be willing to bring cheer into an old-timer's life for just a few moments (it wouldn't take long, believe me). My guess is that the ladies in question could go ahead with whatever they are doing...reading a newspaper, typing a PhD dissertation, making sandwiches, talking to some other guy on a phone-in sex line, hoeing weeds in her garden...while answering some old guy's fondest and maybe final wish. Thank about it. And let me know if you are female and want to do your part to honor your society's elders in a truly meaningful way. I'll find the time if you will. What about your reputation? Good grief, the way my memory works, I won't even remember what the heck we did when I wake up the next morning.

Well, there are memories and then there are memories.... High school reunions are always a bad idea, worse and worse as you get older and older. They become mostly recitations of who has, uh, "passed on," or "organ recitals" of everyone's operations and afflictions. And, is it really a good idea to have a display of "those who have passed on" at reunions? Do we really need to be reminded of our attrition rate? That always puts a glow in a festive evening. I make a point of avoiding reunions. I was really lucky when my high school class had its fiftieth reunion: I got cancer and didn't have to go. The only thing that would have made this self-imposed misery a possibility would have been if I known my old friend and high school classmate Dick Cavett (yes, that Dick Cavett) was planning to be there. The last time we went to a class reunion together he had promised me he wouldn't go if I wouldn't go, and so it was settled: we wouldn't go. But then a week before the scheduled date he called up and said he'd changed his mind...he was going to go, and so should I. So we did.

The thing was predictably painful...everyone but the assholes will tell you that the people who were assholes in high school will still be assholes even 50 years later...except for one thing...Dick Cavett. Dick is obviously the celebrity of our class.

(Famous actress Sandy Dennis who died far too young was in the class right behind us, by the way.) But especially at the time I had some residual celebrity of my own, having written a bunch of books and appearing on national television over a period of 13 years on CBS News "Sunday Morning" as an essayist with Charles Kuralt. At any rate, a point came in the endless evening of the reunion banquet when one of the ladies in attendance asked if she could have her picture taken with us, the two quasi-notables of our high school class. This woman had been gorgeous teenager as a teenager, an object of adolescent lust for both Dick and me. Dick was certainly more popular than I had been in high school but we were neither one of us embraced by the elite. Actually, Dick and I were both more in a class of loners with just a couple friends. And wow, now…here some of the most popular girls in our class…the cheerleaders, the baton twirlers, the rich and socially polished girls of the Country Club set, were asking to have their pictures taken with us.

I was flattered and would have probably just blushed and jumped at the chance, but Dick is far more clever than I. And apparently a good deal meaner too. He said loudly, by way of a general announcement, "Ladies, you can all have your pictures taken with the stars of stage, television, and literature, Roger Welsch and Dick Cavett. Just line up and we'll get started. However…there is one little condition: before you step up in front of the camera, you will have to go over to the microphone and say loudly and clearly, 'When I was in high school, I lusted for Roger Welsch and Dick Cavett.' Everyone laughed. Some of the ladies giggled uncertainly. Surely he was joking. No, surely he wasn't. He actually required each and every one of the fancy girls from our class, ones who wouldn't so much as have looked in our direction fifty years before, step up to the microphone and to the gathered crowd (which of course included in most cases their spouses) say "When I was in high school, I lusted for Roger Welsch and Dick Cavett." It was a moment of supreme triumph. At least for Dick and me.

Linda and I have given some thought to our upcoming 30<sup>th</sup> wedding anniversary…I like to tell people that I've now been married 47 years (counting my first marriage). And Linda hasn't been married at all, at least if the Pope's opinion means anything. She hates that. Anyway, one of the things we considered was redoing our vows, having the big dance and to-do we should have had but couldn't afford when we got married the first time, invite everyone to come and help us celebrate our love. But then we got to thinking, are we really up to dancing more than one or two turns? And wouldn't we probably have to stay up later than 9 o'clock? My biggest concern is that if we did the wedding ceremony again, this time Linda wouldn't show up. Or take way too long to think about it when the preacher asks her if she still takes me for better or worse.

For our wedding night oh-so-many years ago we drove all the way to Grand Island, a full 20 miles from here, and checked in to the Motel 6. In the room next to my folks. Great planning. But Linda has laid down the law and says that for our 30<sup>th</sup> anniversary renewal of our marriage vows, we're going to do things right. She says this time we're going have a fancy meal…maybe supersize at the McDougals, move up from the Motel 6 to the Motel 8, and travel the extra miles to Hastings, another 30 miles down the road. That woman knows how to live crazy.

Most of our occasions for celebrations have taken the same direction. On New Years we now make a point of eating a big meal, lighting some candles, and at the stroke of twelve, share a big kiss, hoot and holler, drink a bottle of champagne and step out onto the dance floor for a few steps. Then we go back home and take our usual noon nap in our recliners.

By way of an equally dramatic contrast to all these good ideas, how about some bad ones? Last week's newspaper here carried a big notice about a "Seniors Expo" to be held at the fairgrounds. Well, okay, I can imagine that an informational, fun get-together for seniors could be a useful sort of thing. And then I read the schedule of events…

8 a.m. Breakfast of weak tea and dry toast with a doctor's review of each attendee's medications protocol

9 a.m. Aerobic exercises designed to help in opening medication containers

9:30 a.m. Rest period (with entertainment by Emil Hldrka and his accordion ensemble)

10:00 a.m. Bingo

11:00 a.m. Rest period

11:30 a.m. Oxygen Clinic (with free bottle recharge) and prostheses maintenance checks and free lube jobs…on the prostheses

12 noon: lunch with bullion soup and crackers, fish cakes, and lime Jell-O with little colored marshmallows and banana slices floating in it.

1 p.m. Bingo

2 p.m. Nap

2:30 p.m. Lawrence Welk Film Festival

3:30 p.m. Bingo and junior high swing choir hymn sing accompanied by seniors rhythm band

4:30 p.m. Leave front door for seniors service van at curb

5:50 p.m. Reach van at curb and depart for retirement centers, nursing homes, and resentful children's spare bedrooms.

While you're at Our Seniors Expo, be sure to visit and patronize our exhibitors!

Jensen's Funeral Home
Chezwicki's Monuments
Watch Your Ps and Qs Urinary Specialists
Full Bore Ambulance and Emergency Medical Services
McAfee's Drive-Thru Surgery Center
Top Value Organ Transplanters (We Buy, Sell, and Trade)
And

Stinky Carl's Big and Tall Mens Diaper Emporium and Septic Service

How can you possibly be depressed when you know your community is putting forth that kind of extra effort for its honored elders?! Here's the moral to that story: When you get to be a Geezer, you're going to have to take care of yourself just as you have done through the first twenty or thirty stages of your life. If you want it done, you're going to have to do it yourself. Especially if you want it done right.

You can't count on someone else (other than me) to get you through the trials of Geezerhood. As usual, you're pretty much going to be on your own, so you're going to have to come up with some strategies to cope. To begin with, stop having birthdays. Nothing is more depressing than lighting the candles on your cake and having the Volunteer Fire Department come roaring into your backyard with hoses opened wide. I called a stop to that nonsense when I turned 50. Now instead of birthdays I celebrate Annual Roger Welsch Recognition Days…all the usual presents and plenty of cake and ice cream, but none of those depressing year counts. This last November we observed the 24th Annual Roger Welsch Recognition Day. Now…there…. Doesn't that sound better than "Roger's 74th birthday? I have developed other useful ways to deal with birthdays, which after the age of 50 do seem to pop up three or four times a year. I don't get out of bed on days that I used to call birthdays. Just stay there, doze, sleep, enjoy a day of complete separation for my regular life. Then I wake up the next day, the 7th of November <u>having not had a birthday!</u> Having had no birthday, you haven't tacked on yet another year onto your age either. You went to bed 72 years old. And you woke up 48 hours later…still 72 years old. It works. Try it. Other age avoidance techniques that have promise are 1) measuring age in dog years…thus I am not 73, but ten and a half years old, and that is increasingly accurate, I might add; or 2) be oh-so modern and go metric. I'm no mathematician so I'll have to leave it up to someone who is to sort that one out.

We were watching something on the History Channel a couple days ago about dinosaurs that died out something like 80 millions years ago and Linda asked, "If dinosaurs have a shelf life, do we humans have one too?" Good question: do we have a "use by…" date? Is there no decent fate for those of us who have less than a couple million dollars stashed in the Bahamas, which we accumulated by not paying our taxes for 50 years? Must we become greeters in box stores? (Linda points out that anyone who believes in the inherent divinity of man has never been in WalMart on a Saturday morning.)

I am conflicted about what to do with senior discounts. I recall how pleased I was and offended at the same time when I was "carded" at the age of 27. Even as a callow youth it was sort of nice to be thought of as callower. But now, do I really want to advertise to that cutie behind the Wendy's counter that I am a geezer? Who knows…maybe she mistakenly thinks I'm only… well, 27. And isn't it flattering when the sloe-eyed beauty scooping popcorn at the movie smiles fetchingly before coyly giving me an extra squirt of butter? And then…how could anyone mistake this move?!…hands me a card indicating that I am now a member of her "extra large" (!) popcorn club and temptingly telling me that if I come back eight more times, she will give me a FREE tub of popcorn. Presumably also with that extra dollop of butter. I detect at least two messages here…maybe more if I were better versed in Freudian interpretation: 1) She wants me to return to her dark corner of the theatre, and 2) she has looked me over and has every expectation that a) I am the kind of big spender who will always go for the extra large tub, and b) I have at least eight more trips to the movies in me. I find that encouraging.

Another way to ease off on responsibility and forget about blame altogether was devised by my Old Man who understood that a time comes when you should continue to go through the motions but don't push it to the point of life being a chore. (As a friend of mine once said when I was surprised by his flirting with a barmaid, "Well, yes…I am married. But I'm not a <u>fanatic</u> about it!") In my father's advanced seniority he still sat down every month with a pocket calculator, paper and pencil, and the month's cancelled checks to balance the family checkbook. Even at the age of 88 and suffering considerable damage from a couple of strokes, he met that paternal obligation. And every month it was the same thing... the checkbook didn't even come close to balancing. He would fuss at it a while, carefully review his figures, try to add them up again and again, and then brilliantly declare "Bank error!" fill in the balance figure provided by the bank, close the damn check account book, stuff it into the desk drawer from which he would pull it again the next month and repeat the same procedure, and move on with his life. Good plan.

If you need some kind of official sanction for the various quirks you develop...perhaps even gladly embrace...in your geezerhood, then simply invent some device to deal with it on your own. No one else is going to do it for you. I have told you already about my Harmless Old Geezer card, something no senior male should ever be without. I have invented two other devices of a similar nature that are indispensable aids for the senior male. The Generic Male Apology, a device useful to men of all ages, is dealt with in detail in my book <u>Love, Sex, and Old Tractors</u>, but briefly the GMA card serves as a cue card for the single most important text a man can ever master other than the most invaluable phrase in marriage: "Yes, dear."

The glue that holds a strong marriage together is the willingness...and speed...of the male in any relationship to issue apologies. I have therefore composed a generic apology that serves almost any purpose:

"Darling, I apologize from the bottom of my soul. I am as sorry as I can be. I don't know why I did something so stupid. You know...I know, I was raised better than this.

Tell me what I can do to make this up to you, if anything possibly can. I swear I will do my best never to do anything this stupid again. You know I love you and only do such things out of ignorance, never on purpose. Please accept my heartfelt apology. Let me take you out to supper and a movie tonight..."

The thing is, you don't even really need to know what it is you've done. If you are any kind of man at all and if you have had any sort of continuing contact with a woman in your life, you simply <u>know</u> you have done <u>something</u> you need to apologize for. I recommend that every man memorize this generic apology to the point where he can recite it even under the tension of being discovered <u>flagrante delicto</u> with even the worst kind of delicto, if you catch my drift. In fact, mornings before I come downstairs to make my morning coffee, I just yell the MGA down the stairs in Linda's direction to lay a solid apologetic base for the day and to cover whatever I might have been found guilty of during the night…you know, some indiscretion I committed in one of her dreams. Or more likely, in one of mine.

The main thing about Geezerhood when it comes to regrets and apologies, as far as I'm concerned, is that you don't wind up having to make apologies to yourself for having missed chances. I'm not thinking of any particular chances, just that it seems to me that regret in your senior years is just about the saddest thing I can imagine because way too soon you reach a point where there's no making up for what you've missed. You should have climbed that mountain, you should have taken that white-water rafting trip, you should have spent a week fishing with the Old Man, you should have taken that hot-air balloon flight, you should have… Well, you get the idea.

Generally speaking, I have pretty much responded to my own urges and yens and not passed up a lot of chances. There are some things I wish I could do again…I'd love to spend a month or ten in Qaanaaq, Greenland, far above the Arctic Circle, for example. I'd like to snorkel the reef off of Akumal in Mexico's Yucatan again. I'd like to take another spin in a formula car at a racing school. I'd like to spend another night sleeping on a round bed with satin sheets between Naomi Campbell and Heather Locklear. Okay… okay… so the bets are still out on that last one; I'm sure it's just a matter of those two ladies being too busy answering other mail so they haven't gotten to <u>my</u> letter yet.…

For twenty years I stewed about wanting a tattoo in recognition of one of the proudest recognitions of my life, my adoption into the Omaha Indian Tribe. It was finally my beloved Linda who took care of those arrangements and took me to a tattoo parlor for the first time in my life, well into my 60s, 35 years after the occasion of my adoption into the Omaha Tribe, to get the tattoo, a device to remind me regularly of the lessons of constant gratitude that gift of brotherhood gave me.

Then I worried about how I was going to explain this self-mutilation to my parents. Yes, I was already 60 years old, scarcely a teenager, and my folks were well into their 80s, but still...I knew they wouldn't approve. The day came when I was visiting them in their apartment, I saw Dad look quizzically at the back of my left hand, and then...then...the dreaded question: "Rog...what the heck is that on the back of your hand?"

I said, "A tattoo, Dad," and held it up for his inspection, awaiting the inevitable scorn and disapproval. He looked at it a moment and then stunned me...as he often did...by saying, "You know, I always wanted a tattoo. But they cost two dollars, and I didn't have two dollars."

See? I could have not gotten a tattoo to avoid Dad's disapproval. And sooner or later...I would have regretted it. (I have since added four more tattoos, the three the Lovely Carla gave me to help her aim her radiation accelerator at my nethers, and another to symbolize my adoption a couple years ago by my Lakota brother, Chashasha. I wasn't about to wait 35 years to get this one! And I certainly wasn't going to forgo it and live years regretting the omission. In fact, think of what joy I could have spread if I had invited Dad to go with me and have a tattoo of his own on my expense.

Another device of my invention is not just for senior males but might also be useful for younger men. But the thing is, somehow men when they reach their dotage often get a little more daring, partially driven by the pressures of ALC (Advanced Life Crises) or by the genuinely honest appreciation of the fact that they can go ahead and take the risk because they will 1) be perceived as incapable of actually carrying out any threat of a dalliance and 2) probably are indeed incapable of actually carrying out any threat of a dalliance.

This is my WVW, or Wedding Vow Waiver. And again in all honesty, it is more Linda's invention than mine. In an effort to make my hahahahahahaha Golden Years less painful, she felt she could give me more latitude without actually giving her—or me—cause to worry about anything particular or questionable actually coming of it all, things being what they are, me being what I am, etc. The card is as follows—

WEDDING VOW WAIVER......
(Name)

is hereby released from his wedding vows

from (date & time)

to (date & time)

Please return him to (address)

Preferably not before the stated time. [This addition to the card is Linda's idea, I might note.] Please don't let him hurt himself.
(Signed) Approving Spouse:

I have yet to find a situation where I could use my WVW card but who knows? I'm prepared if the occasion arises, among other things. And that's the idea of it...

Well, at least that's a good part of the idea of it. The buried message is actually that Linda is still in charge. She's the one who gives the permission because she knows she can. And that I can't. Which brings up another enormous factor in Geezerhood: Men are geezers; Women are rarely, if ever Geezers. Which means that like good wine, nothing tests and refines marriage like age. And now I'm not kidding. Not at all. Geezerhood is when a good marriage really counts.

My parents were a very traditional, peasant product. They were first generation Americans, raised in a society of migrant laborers, doing hard work at low wages. They turned their pay envelopes over to their parents up to and including the week they were married. They worked hard all their lives, never forgetting the hard times of the Great Depression and the World War. They were German through and through as am I. Dad ruled our household. What he said, went. He was the boss. He was appalled once to see me in a car being driven by a woman: the man drives the car. He earned the money and he managed the money. He was the Lord of the Manor.

And I believed that.

There were certainly moments when Mom's power surfaced, but never in anything but the most subtle of ways. There is a joke out here in the rural west that a man gets married so he can have someone to open the gates, the custom being that a man drives the pickup up to a farm fence gate and then the passenger gets out, opens the gate, waits until the driver goes through, and then closes the gate again behind the vehicle.

That's the way things worked in my family. Dad always drove, so when he and Mom came up to the garage door, she got out and lifted the large, old-fashioned wooden garage door. But the day Dad retired, Mom announced that since he was no longer the breadwinner in the outfit, the least he could do is open the blasted garage door himself and let her drive the car in. I wasn't there for that discussion so I can't imagine how the conversation went, but the outcome was that he conceded the wheel and did indeed become the one who got out and lifted the garage door.

For one week. His discovery of the weight and clumsiness of that damn door must have come to him as something of a surprise because at the end of the first week of the new arrangement, Dad called Sears and had them install a remotely controlled garage door opener. I don't know if that means he lost the battle but actually won the war but I do know he had to listen to Mom tell that story for all the remaining 20 years of his life.

When Dad got into his seventies, I started to notice things about my parents' marriage, things I hadn't noticed before. And even more so when he entered his eighties and had some major

health     problems…heart     attacks,     strokes,     advancing
Alzheimer's… It wasn't as if anything new was happening within
their relationship; I simply started to get the feeling that what had
always been there was somehow becoming more visible. What I
was just newly seeing left me with the unavoidable conclusion
that…well…Mom was in charge. And in fact had always been in
charge. She was the strength and force in their union. She was
running things. It's not that she was now flaunting control or
exerting more control or even revealing her control. She had not
been some kind of domestic subversive all those years; she hadn't
undermined Dad's authority. Actually, quite to the contrary, out
of her love she had always deferred to him. She was now and
always had been so circumspect and gentle in her exercise of
power that no one… including me, and I suspect Dad… even
noticed. Considering the circumstances of Dad's decreasing
powers, she simply couldn't now hide the reality that she was in
charge.

Then I recalled that, well, of course…whenever a boy I
wanted something from a car to a trip, I would ask Dad, he would
say he'd think about it, or even just say no. And I would wait.
And I might take my case to Mom, not ever thinking of asking
her to contradict Dad or go to bat for me against him, but simply
to tell her my situation. And then a week or two later Dad would
announce that he'd made his decision. Or changed his mind. And
that he was willing to go along with my plan. And it happened
that way with every issue. As Dad's physical and mental
problems became worse, Mom's leadership became not stronger
but more visible. It was also clear that the new visibility of her
strength was not a power play on her part, but a concession to
reality. Not only was she not taking over, she continued to insist
that Dad was in charge…even when he clearly was not. Her
acquiescence to his titular dominance was not patronizing or
fearful but a clear expression and exercise of her love and respect
for him. It was touching to see her take any and all business
matters to him for his review and approval even though he didn't
have the slightest idea what he was looking at, or sometimes even

who she was. Again, her procedural deference to him was not a matter of anything at all but an expression of love and respect. She wanted to continue letting him have his dignity, and she did that until his dying day. We should all be so lucky as to have a mate like that, huh? However that may be, one thing we can do to encourage that kind gentility in our own lives and that's to be a mate like that.

I'm a firm advocate of marriage…not for everyone, to be sure, but certainly for me. At least as long as I have someone as fine as Linda by my side. Marriage is great for children and the activities leading up to children, for showing off your studly accomplishments, for cookery and cleanery, for…well, you know…all the reasons one gets married for in youth. But I can tell you for a fact that marriage is never more critical than when you when you step across the threshold into Geezerhood. At that point the emotional support is more important than ever before, more important than you can imagine. I have come to realize that all those first 30 years of our marriage, raising Antonia, struggling to make a living, making huge…and sometimes radical decisions, like leaving a good job and the city to move out here to the rural countryside and live on my good looks… All that was only preparation for the real rewards and meaning of marriage, our time now when we have come to understand and appreciate our partnership, understanding, mutual dependence, trust, humor, and yep, that same old word we started with so long ago…love.

And that's not just the case for Geezers of the masculine persuasion but for anyone who intends to get older. I suppose I could face the various vicissitudes of ageing on my own, and so could Linda face those of hers, but I'm sure glad I don't have to go at it that way. We went together this morning to another appointment with the oncologist…everything seems to be going well… and I was a bit nervous about it. Linda sensed that and said on our drive there that if the doctor asked about the condition of my erections these days, she was going to say that everything seemed fine to her but she'd noticed that the hired girl had been complaining a bit now and then. And with that, my anxiety about what the doctor would actually say dissolved in at least a moment's worth of laughter.

There's a lot of embarrassment in Geezerhood, or at least there could be if I didn't have someone like Linda to laugh with. I once read somewhere that everyone is either a nurse or a patient in life, but I would argue that we are all both, sometimes a nurse, sometimes a patient. In Geezerhood, in a happy…or at least successful…marriage, you pretty much have to be both all the time. I guess if I had one piece of advice for all you Geezers or incipient Geezers out there, it would be, "Get yourself a companion and friend like Linda." Laugh when the joke is hers, joke when she's the one who needs the laugh.

No doubt about it, while Geezerhood is a tough time of life. Or can be. It is a time when friends become all the more important. And a time when there is a much greater appreciation for the blessing that good friends can be. I have found that I have less and less time for people who aren't friends and a real desire to spend more time with those who are. It's not just a matter of being sick or even just old; it seems to me that it's a matter of finally recognizing what is important in life… like good friends. There's no other medicine like it. So gather your friends and family around you, and if you are only watching geezerhood from a distance and having a ways to go to get there yourself, take a clue from Native Americans, from whom we should have learned a lot over the centuries anyway…and respect your elders for little more than that they have become elders. It's not all that easy, after all. But, now that I think about it, it's not all that hard either.

I find there can also be a renewed comfort in solitude. Especially in marriage. I am confident of Linda's love and I hope she is confident of mine because she has every reason to be. I can't imagine a better partner and friend…even though as often as not these days we may spend our evenings apart but in the same house, she watching her television shows and I watching mine. As I explained to a friend earlier to day, it's a matter of

"Deadwood" upstairs and "Desperate Housewives" downstairs. [Pause. Think about it....think about it...think about it...now!... laugh!]

I used that line a couple hours ago on one of my best friends, Dick Day. And now I can't get him to stop laughing. Is he laughing at me, or with me? Who cares? He's laughing, and that's what counts. Good friends are like that.

# An afternote—

As of this writing I am just back from another visit to the cardiac ward of our local hospital. There was good news and bad news: the good news is that they went in, took a look and found nothing. The bad news is, they went in, took a look, and found nothing. So I came home with nothing more than a very sore groin, a limp, and the same old, tired instructions—"Lose weight, get more exercise, reduce stress, and pay this bill on time." No, that's not quite right: I came home with a renewed spirit of humiliation. After the procedure I was lying there in the recovery room and every ten minutes for the rest of the day yet another young, pretty woman came in (not one male!), without so much as an introduction hoisted the hem of my gown, poked around with her cold fingers, and said...no kidding, "Beautiful! Beautiful! Still nice and soft!" I tried to respond accordingly by replying, "Well, young lady, you should have known me when I was younger." And then there was the customary line, "Oh Mr. Welsch, you're so cute. You remind me of my grandpa."

As I noted before, I suspect that nurses are taught that line in one of the first classes they take in nursing school, but this time I found out more about those classes and was stopped dead in my smart-alecky tracks. I told this story to my daughter Joyce, whose friend Shawn just had a similar cardiac procedure in another city and she reported with similar surprise that…the nurses in that hospital had done and said <u>precisely the same thing</u>! "Beautiful! Beautiful! Still nice and soft!" Now I know, if not the rest of the story, at least more of it: that too is a standard nurse line dedicated to shredding whatever sense of pride and dignity a male patient might have left after donning the backless gown, being shaved in dangerous proximity to tender nethers, and having total strangers move and shuffle things around down there as if they were mixing up Scrabble tiles. I feel used. And cheap. And now I will forever live with doubts…is my groin really double beautiful? I'll never know, at least not until I do lose a lot of weight.